D0911308

The Discovery
at the Dragon's Mouth

The Famous JUDY BOLTON *Mystery Stories*

By MARGARET SUTTON

In Order of Publication

A JUDY BOLTON Mystery

The Discovery
at the Dragon's
Mouth

BY
Margaret Sutton

Illustrated by Pelagie Doane

APPLEWOOD BOOKS
Bedford, Massachusetts

The Discovery at the Dragon's Mouth
was originally published in 1960.

Reprinted by permission of the estate of Margaret Sutton.
All Rights Reserved.

For a complete list of titles in the Judy Bolton Mysteries,
please visit judybolton.awb.com.

Thank you for purchasing an Applewood Book.
Applewood reprints America's lively classics—books from
the past that are still of interest to modern readers.
For a free copy of our current catalog, write to:

Applewood Books
P.O. Box 365
Bedford, MA 01730
www.awb.com

ISBN 978-1-4290-9051-3

MANUFACTURED IN THE U.S.A.

Honey banged frantically at the door

A Judy Bolton Mystery

THE DISCOVERY
AT THE
DRAGON'S MOUTH

By

Margaret Sutton

Grosset & Dunlap

PUBLISHERS   NEW YORK

To
LAUREL *and* LINDA
who also explored the possibilities
of dinosaur riding

The Discovery at the Dragon's Mouth

Contents

Contents

CHAPTER I

The Strangers Arrive

"I'M NOT at all sure I like the idea of renting our house to perfect strangers," mused Judy.

She stood on the landing of the attic stairs—right in the way of Horace and Peter, who were moving a chest of drawers from the second to the third floor.

"Try tilting it," Peter suggested, ignoring Judy's complaint.

"Too big," Horace said, panting. "We'll have to heave it up over the railing."

"Okay. Here goes!"

Judy stepped quickly aside. So did her cat, Black-berry. He seemed to disapprove of what was going on even more than his mistress did. She gathered him into her arms and stroked his velvety black fur.

"You know we're going away again, don't you, Blackberry?" she crooned. "That means leaving you with Mother and Dad in Farringdon. Horace, if you'd get rid of that parrot—"

"The parrot stays. He's good company," her brother interrupted before Judy could finish.

"I've heard of worse pets," Peter said. "Dragons, for instance."

"Dragons?" asked Judy.

Peter Dobbs, the young FBI agent she had married, answered, "There used to be land dragons—what we call dinosaurs. When I've finished this refresher course in Washington," he added mysteriously, "I may be asked to explore the possibilities of dinosaur riding."

"It sounds like fun. Will I be a cavewoman?" asked Judy. "I wonder if I can play the part."

"There will be a part for someone to play, but it will be dangerous. I'm going to try and keep you out of this."

"Please, Peter!" begged Judy.

Horace sighed. "I've heard this routine before. You may as well give up, Peter, and let Sis in on your secrets. *She* doesn't need any refresher course. She has a natural talent for mysteries."

Judy made a face at her brother. She didn't want him teasing Peter because he had to go back to school.

The government expected its agents to go back every six weeks or so for field training in firearms. A two-weeks refresher course was also required about a year after initial training. This was the course Peter would soon be taking.

"I suppose I should try and keep out of trouble for a change," Judy agreed. "We'll have trouble enough with strangers moving into our house."

"Strangers!" Horace exclaimed in mock surprise. "My dear sister, haven't you heard that in the ideal community there are no strangers? We are all one great big human family."

"In that case," Judy said tartly, "I'm afraid I don't trust all the members of it. Bank robbers, for instance. Why, only last week a masked gunman walked into the Farringdon National Bank. If the teller hadn't obeyed him when he asked her to fill a paper bag with money—"

"She would have been shot on the spot. I know," Horace broke in. "I reported the story for the *Farringdon Daily Herald*, as usual."

Judy could not resist adding, "And, as usual, the gunman got away. How do we know he isn't the very man who's renting our house for the summer?"

"How convenient if he should be!" Horace laughed. "Peter could nab him and collect the reward—"

"You know we aren't allowed to accept rewards, Horace," Peter reminded him.

"There are rewards and rewards. Turning in a wanted man is a reward in itself. You protect society. You uphold democracy——"

"Just uphold your end of this chest of drawers, Horace," Peter said. "Where do you want it, Judy?"

"At the end of my sewing room, I guess."

"In front of the window?"

"Yes, please. I'll draw the curtains." Judy sighed. "We won't be looking out."

Peter looked at her with inquiring blue eyes. "Aren't you glad about the trip, Angel? You've told me dozens of times you wished you could go to Washington with me. Dry Brook Hollow is pretty lonesome. You've said so yourself. You've even imagined your grandmother's ghost haunting the place."

"I didn't," Judy began to protest, but it was no use. "It's just the way I feel about attics," she explained. "There were voices and things in the attic in Farringdon, and this one is still filled with Grandma's things. I never did find time to sort them."

Judy didn't know why, but the prospect of sorting her grandmother's things suddenly appealed to her more than the trip to Washington. She walked over to the storeroom and peered in. "Treasures," she said. "Grandma's treasures of the past. It's like breaking a promise to her to go off and leave them with strangers. Suppose there is a fire. The attic door will be locked. Nobody could get up here to save anything."

"Leave it open then," Peter suggested. "The Wheatleys aren't arsonists. They aren't strangers, either," he continued. "I went to law school with Bob Wheatley and know him well. You remember his wife, don't you, Judy? She used to be children's librarian in Roulsville before the flood."

"Do you mean Miss Pringle? Did she get married? Will wonders never cease! Maud Pringle was a typical old maid if I ever saw one," declared Judy. "It's hard for me to believe she's Maud Wheatley now. I wonder if she still looks as if she'd been eating sour prunes. She did have a cute younger sister who married a gangster."

"You've got it all wrong, Sis," Horace objected. "That cute little blonde you have in mind is her brother's wife, Peggy Pringle. It is Harry Pringle, Maud's brother, who's in trouble with the law. He's a wanted man, isn't he, Peter?"

"We would like to locate him and ask him some questions," Peter admitted. "His car was last seen leaving the Rapid City Bank right after a holdup. Apparently he and his wife abandoned their little boy. The Wheatleys have him now."

"They do?" Judy's gray eyes widened. The redheaded daughter of Dr. Bolton could scent another mystery. "Can't we find out what really happened to his parents?"

"Perhaps." Peter gave Judy a searching look. "Bob

tells me the little boy isn't very truthful. I'm afraid the best we can do is help provide a home for him and maybe a little of the happiness a boy that age deserves. He's only six."

Now Judy was really curious. "Where did he live before? Were his parents traveling with him? Where is Rapid City, anyway? When was the bank robbed?"

"Last September," replied Peter, answering Judy's final question first.

"I don't remember seeing anything about it in the papers. What's the matter, Horace?" Judy asked teasingly. "Doesn't the *Farringdon Daily Herald* cover *all* the news?"

"We do our best," he answered, "but if you will remember, there was a lot of local news last September. We can't give valuable space on the front page to a bank that's robbed way out west. Rapid City is in South Dakota, or didn't you know?"

Judy had to confess that she didn't know nearly as much about the United States as she would like to. She had crossed the country only once by train, flying back and not seeing much scenery, because of bad weather. The trip to Washington would be different, she hoped. This time they were to travel by car.

"We'll stop off and see some of the sights, won't we?" Judy asked later, when the chest was in place and their personal belongings all packed away in it.

Peter said he hoped there would be time for a little

sightseeing. Soon after Horace left, Judy went to her bedroom and began packing a few things she thought she would need in Washington. It was apt to be chilly this early in the spring.

"I'll need a warm coat," she decided, making mental notes as the pile of folded clothing in her suitcase grew higher, "and a suit with plenty of fresh blouses. My camera, too! There should be pictures. Oh, Peter," she called, "I wish—"

Judy's wish was not expressed. At that moment a car was heard driving down their private road. It rumbled across the bridge and stopped before the house. Judy ran to the window to watch beside Blackberry, who was sitting on the window sill.

"Come on, Kevin," she heard the former Miss Pringle command in the same sharp voice she had used in reprimanding noisy children in the library. "This is where we're going to live."

The boy she called Kevin needed no urging. He raced ahead of his aunt and uncle right across the flower bed where Judy's perennials were sending up little green shoots.

"Peter! They're here." Judy was suddenly all a-tremble. Kevin was crying out excitedly.

"Look, Uncle Bob! It's a spooky house. See? There's a cat in the window. I want the cat, Auntie Maud. Can I keep the cat? Please, please let me keep him! He's just like my old Bumper."

CHAPTER II

A Stolen Teddy Bear

AFTER greetings had been exchanged, almost the first question Maud Wheatley asked Judy was, "Does the cat go with the house?"

"Oh, no, he's my cat," Judy protested quickly.

"Will you leave him here? We'll take good care of him," Bob Wheatley promised.

It was a generous offer, and yet Judy couldn't bring herself to agree to it. "I—I planned to take him over to Mother's," she began.

"Oh, please leave him! I like black cats," Kevin declared. "I'll be good to him." He looked into the cat's great green eyes and said, "You like me, don't you, Bumper?"

"His name is Blackberry, not Bumper," Judy informed the little boy in a voice that Peter told her later sounded almost haughty.

"Can I call him Blackie?"

"He won't like it," Peter prophesied. "He's a dignified cat and likes to be treated with respect."

Everybody laughed except Judy. She didn't think it was funny. She didn't want to rent the house to the Wheatleys or any other family. But the house was already rented for the whole summer—perhaps longer. Only the things in the attic were safely stored away. Judy had left the door unlocked. It seemed better that way. But her heart was filled with misgivings. Reluctantly she showed the Wheatley family the rooms they would occupy.

"Such beautiful, spacious rooms!" Maud Wheatley exclaimed. "I like a kitchen fireplace, and the living room is so inviting with all those books and the big window seat. Mrs. Dobbs, you have exquisite taste. Such priceless antiques! Where did you find them?"

"This was my grandmother's home," Judy said quietly. "Most of them were hers—and they are priceless."

"Your grandmother was Mrs. Smeed? Then you are Judy Bolton, the little girl who used to come to the library for the Oz books?"

Judy couldn't help smiling at the memory. "Yes, I read every one of them. I read everything—even

Grandma's dictionary. That's it over there by the window seat. You—you won't let Kevin tear it, will you?"

The little boy drew himself up to his full height. "I don't tear things," he announced, and Judy felt ashamed. She must do something to make these people feel welcome even if her heart wasn't in it. She turned to Kevin and asked, "Would you like to see the barn?"

"Oh," he exclaimed, his eyes round with excitement, "is there a barn?"

Judy told him that there certainly was.

"Yes, and a horse and cow to go with it," Peter added. "And you can ride Ginger," he continued. "He used to be pretty frisky, but he's calmed down in the last year or two."

"He nearly killed me once," Judy said ruefully.

"I'll like living in a house with a real barn," Kevin spoke up. "When I traveled with Mommy and Daddy, we stayed in tourist camps. We were on our way to Yellowstone. Daddy said I'd see bears just like Bumper. Why didn't he take me to see the bears, Auntie Maud? Where is my daddy? And why did Mommy go away and leave me? Aren't we ever going to Yellowstone?"

"One question at a time, Kevin. I don't know why your daddy didn't take you to see the bears," Mrs. Wheatley answered, "and no, we aren't ever going to

Yellowstone. The hot springs are dangerous, and the bears have been known to claw people. I shouldn't think you'd want to go there."

"I do want to," he insisted. "Daddy had it all planned. He didn't think it was dangerous. He had money enough—"

"I'll bet he had." Bob Wheatley said this between his teeth. He and his wife looked at each other.

"Tell me about your daddy. Perhaps I can find him for you," Peter suggested.

"Will you find Bumper, too?"

"I'll try," Peter promised.

He listened closely to the little fellow's chatter as they left for a tour of the grounds. There were chickens to see as well as the horse and cow. Kevin promised faithfully that he would feed the chickens. Nothing more was said about Blackberry until Judy and Peter were ready to leave. Apparently Kevin thought it was all settled.

"I'll take good care of the cat," he promised earnestly. "I like him. He's soft and furry, and I can whisper secrets to him just the way I used to whisper things to Bumper."

Curiosity got the better of Judy. "Who is Bumper?" she asked. "You've mentioned him several times."

"He's a bear." Kevin paused, looking first at his uncle and then at his aunt. "Shall I tell them?" he asked.

"You may tell them the truth," Mrs. Wheatley replied in the severe voice she used to use when she was Miss Pringle.

"I did—"

"Never mind," Bob Wheatley interrupted. "I'll tell them about Bumper. He was a Teddy bear. Kevin was very fond of him, apparently, and then he lost him."

"I didn't," Kevin protested. "I wouldn't lose Bumper. I kept him right with me all the time just the way Daddy told me to. I took him to bed the same as always. I didn't lose him. A bad man came in the middle of the night and stole him."

Bob Wheatley laughed. "Did you ever hear of a grown man stealing a Teddy bear? It's as bad as that dinosaur ride."

"But Daddy did let me ride on a dinosaur," Kevin insisted.

"Where was this?"

"On a hill with lots of dinosaurs."

"See what I mean?" Bob Wheatley said to Peter. "How can anyone get the truth from a boy who tells such ridiculous stories?"

Now Judy knew what Peter had meant when he said he might be asked to explore the possibilities of dinosaur riding. Apparently he did not think the stories were so ridiculous.

"Can you describe this man who stole your Teddy bear, Kevin?" Peter asked.

"He was black and furry, and he had little ears that

stood up like your cat's ears," Kevin began. "My daddy told me to put a candy heart in him to make him alive—"

"Mr. Dobbs asked you to describe the man, not the Teddy bear," Maud Wheatley interrupted.

"I didn't see him very well," the little boy admitted.

His uncle laughed again. "You've heard of the little man who wasn't there? He always steals the things small boys lose. He used to steal my caps regularly until my mother gave up and let me go bareheaded. He's a real criminal, he is. Now he's stolen Kevin's Teddy bear."

"Was the bear black? Teddy bears are usually brown," Judy put in.

"This one," said Mrs. Wheatley, "was an unusual bear. It was made out of black caracul except for its face, which was made of leather. Far too expensive a toy, I told Harry, for a child. But my brother always did buy expensive things. He used to bring me gifts—"

There was an awkward silence. Nobody mentioned the bank that had been robbed or the fact that Kevin's parents had abandoned him.

"Poor little fellow," thought Judy. "He needs something to comfort him." But still she couldn't bring herself to offer Blackberry.

"I know I'm selfish," she said to Peter a few minutes later, as she helped him pile suitcases into the car. "It's just that—that I'm so afraid we'll come home and find the house a shambles. Frankly, I don't like the Wheatleys. Ol' Miss Pringle, as we used to call her, hasn't changed a bit. She never did understand children, and I can see she doesn't understand Kevin any better than she did the children who used to come to the library. What do you suppose made her become a librarian in the first place?"

"Maybe it was a love of books, not children. It's Bob Wheatley who surprises me," declared Peter. "He laughs at the wrong things."

Judy shook her head. "I see what you mean. What do you think about leaving Blackberry with them, Peter?"

"I think it would be best," he replied gently. "Kevin is a lonely little boy, and a cat, as you and I both know, can be a good companion."

"He needs a Teddy bear, not a cat." Judy was almost in tears. "I'm foolishly fond of Blackberry. I won't have him teased and pushed around."

But when Peter put it that way, Judy knew it was right for her to leave Blackberry. He didn't seem to mind. She gave him a parting pat on the head, and he continued to purr as contentedly as ever.

"That cat loves the house better than he does us, anyway," she told Peter as she climbed in the car beside him.

Blackberry was still sitting on the window sill. His ears went up as if he heard something. Then Judy heard it, too.

"The telephone!" she exclaimed. "Peter, do you think we ought to go back and answer it?"

CHAPTER III

Abandoned

AFTERWARDS Judy was almost sorry they hadn't let the telephone ring. Peter did go back to answer it. He talked with someone in Washington for about ten minutes. When he returned to the car he told Judy all their plans would have to be changed.

"Just drive me to the airport," he said. "I'm sorry, Angel. But we haven't time to drive down leisurely the way we planned. The chief has one more assignment for me before school begins. He wants me in Washington this evening. I didn't argue. His orders come first."

"What about me?" asked Judy. "I don't want to drive down to Washington all alone."

"Here's the way I have it figured out," Peter told her as they sped on toward Farringdon. "I won't have much time to spend with you during the week anyway. Classes will take up most of the day, and it looks as if there will be a few evening sessions as well. Why don't you wait until Saturday and drive down with Horace and Honey? My sister deserves a little trip, and your brother never objects to taking her. They can come back by bus or train after they've seen the sights. If Horace is in a hurry to get back, they can fly."

"But this is Monday! What do I do in the meantime?" Judy asked, dismayed. "I haven't any house, or any cat——"

"You and Honey will think of something," Peter broke in cheerfully. "And you can stay at your mother's. I'm sorry, Angel, but that's the way it has to be. Honey's vacation is coming up soon. She spoke of a trip to New York——"

"But I've just been there."

The New York trip did not appeal to Judy until she thought of her little namesake, Judy Irene Meredith, and the kitten she had promised her.

"I know what I'll do," she decided. "I'll call up Helen Brandt and see if those kittens her cat was expecting are big enough to be given away. She told me I could have my choice."

"Do that," Peter said as if the gift of a kitten would

solve all Judy's problems. Sometimes, she felt, he seemed to forget that she was no longer a little girl. He just didn't seem to realize how much she wanted to be with him and share in his work the way she used to when they worked together in the little law office in Roulsville.

At the airport, a brick building flanked by two enormous hangars, Judy kissed Peter good-bye and watched him walk up the wheeled ramp and into the big silver-winged plane that would take him to Washington without her. Now she knew how Kevin felt, abandoned by his parents.

"I feel abandoned, too," she thought. "Uncle Sam is taking Peter away from me. It isn't just the school. It's afterwards. He can't even talk about his assignments most of the time. And I'm the one who likes to solve mysteries!"

It seemed suddenly unfair. "Why was I born a girl, anyway?" Judy asked herself. "I don't like the things girls are supposed to do—housework and sewing." She thought of her sewing room with the big chest in front of the window. She thought of the Wheatleys living in the house her grandmother had left her, and half hoped the old lady would come back and haunt it. "I'm selfish! Selfish!" she scolded herself, but her feeling about sharing the house with strangers didn't change.

Here in the waiting room at the airport she was

surrounded by strangers who had just come in on the plane Peter was taking. As soon as they claimed their luggage most of them hurried toward waiting taxis or private cars. The air buzzed with greetings.

As Judy moved toward the telephone booth to call Helen and ask about the kittens, she caught a scrap of conversation.

"He was supposed to meet me here. I expected him to come in on this plane."

"Why don't you have him paged?"

The first speaker, a small, dark girl who had been waiting for some time, said she hadn't thought of that and thanked the information clerk.

A moment later a voice boomed over the loud-speaker. "Paging Mr. Nogard! Paging Mr. Nogard! Will Charles Nogard please come to the information booth?"

The girl who was having him paged was wearing a corsage on her suit lapel. Judy thought at first they were orchids, but when she looked more closely she could see that they were snapdragons tied with a yellow net ribbon.

"Snapdragons aren't very expensive," she thought. "I'll call the florist and have him make up a corsage like that for me. I won't feel so abandoned if I'm wearing flowers."

Judy found a telephone and ordered the corsage. Then, out of curiosity, she waited until the dark girl

left the airport. Mr. Nogard evidently was not going
to appear.

Then Judy drove over to the Brandt estate without
calling Helen. Fortunately she found her young friend
at home busy at her desk with a stack of schoolbooks
at her side. In the corner behind the desk her cat,
Tabby, was sleeping underneath a pile of well-fed kittens.

"Aren't they darling?" Helen exclaimed, showing
them to Judy. "Look! They're all colors. Two are
yellow like Tabby. Two are calico, and the other two
are black."

"Oh, good!" Judy pounced on one of the little black
ones. "May I have him?" she asked. "You promised—"

"You may have them all," declared Helen. "Mother
says I have to get rid of them."

"All six?" Judy was aghast. "Helen, I couldn't possibly take six kittens. What would I do with them?"

"You could find homes for them, couldn't you?
Please try," Helen pleaded. "You have lots of friends.
There's Lois and Lorraine—"

"Lorraine doesn't like cats," Judy interrupted. "I
will ask some of my other friends, though. Holly Pot-
ter is my nearest neighbor in Dry Brook Hollow. She
might want a kitten, and I'm almost sure Honey
would. Old Checker, the mother of Blackberry, died
of old age. Grandpa and Grandma Dobbs might like
another calico cat. They could call this one Chessie."

"You'll take three, then?"

"Two will be enough," declared Judy. "I'll be back if I want any more."

She left hurriedly with the kittens in a shoebox, not even glancing back at the fountain she had once felt sure must be haunted. Only the Farringdon-Pett estate and this more secluded country home of the Brandt family boasted fountains. The showplaces of Farringdon were fast being replaced by more modern homes or by apartment buildings.

Judy's next stop was the apartment in downtown Farringdon where Grandpa and Grandma Dobbs had lived ever since the Roulsville flood washed away their former home. The Bolton family, too, had moved to Farringdon, and it was here that Judy finished high school and went to business college, becoming Peter's first secretary. She had married him while she was still in her teens. "Too young," people said, shaking their heads. Even Grandpa and Grandma Dobbs thought Judy was too young for the responsibilities of marriage and hovered over her as if she were a child. The old people were both at home.

"Well, if it isn't our Judy!" exclaimed Grandpa, pleased as always, to see her. "Where's Peter? I hear he's taking you away from us again."

"He's away," Judy said. "I just saw him off on a plane to Washington, but he couldn't take me."

"Government business, I suppose?"

"Yes," Judy said, beginning to feel abandoned again. "Renting our house wasn't such a good idea after all. Now I'll have to stay with Mother and Dad until—"

A faint mew from the box she was holding interrupted her. Grandpa Dobbs lifted the cover.

"Whew!" he exclaimed. "I thought you had Blackberry cooped up in a box. That would never do."

"Land sakes alive! Where'd you get the kittens? This little one is just like our old Checker," clucked Grandma, lifting the small calico cat out of the box and cradling it in her apron. "Is it old enough to leave its mother? What's its name?"

"*Her* name," said Judy, "is Chessie. First you had Checker and now Chess. Grandpa likes the game, and if you like the kitten she's yours. The other one is a male. I think little Judy will want to name it Blackberry after its father. The problem is, how will I deliver it?"

Grandpa Dobbs considered this question for a moment. Then, chuckling, he said, "I think I have it. You and Honey can deliver the cat. Honey's bound and determined to spend her vacation in New York or some other far-off place. Do her good to get away from the old folks, I told her. The last thing Grandma and I want to do is tie her down. We're both well. We'll be fine here by ourselves while you and Honey take a little trip. It's about time."

"Take a trip?" echoed Judy.

"Why not?" asked Grandpa. "Honey's been slaving over that drawing board long enough. She's been saving for a real vacation. Says she wants to take her sketchbook along and draw what she likes for a change, not just what Mr. Dean tells her."

Judy could understand that. Honey was a creative artist. Too much of her work for the Dean Studio was copying other people's designs on stencils.

"Will she want me along?" Judy began. "I mean, if she's going to take her sketchbook."

"Why don't you ask her?" Grandpa Dobbs suggested. "She went out shopping, but she ought to be back soon. Look—here she is now!"

CHAPTER IV

A Corsage of Snapdragons

THE door had flown open, and in came Honey, the mystery girl of Judy's high school days and now her sister-in-law and dearest chum. The two girls hugged each other and then stood back, each admiring the other's clothes.

They were dressed almost alike in trim spring suits. Honey was wearing a bright orange sweater that brought out the highlights in her honey-colored hair. Her suit was a tweedy brown.

Judy's gray suit and green sweater were perfect for a gray-eyed redhead. Her eyes changed color, she had been told, to match what she was wearing. Today they were almost green.

Gray-green eyes looked into blue ones with deep affection.

"Judy, how glad I am to see you!" Honey exclaimed. "What happened? I thought you and Peter were on your way to Washington by now."

Judy explained how their plans had been changed. She tried to make her voice sound cheerful, but it was no use. Honey knew her too well not to see through her play-acting.

"You're disappointed, aren't you?" Honey said sympathetically. "I know I would be. I hate to plan things and then have something turn up at the last minute to change my plans. Sometimes, though, the new plans turn out to be better than the old ones. So let's start making them, shall we?"

"You are a—a Honey!" Judy burst out gratefully, and they both laughed and hugged each other again.

"I intended to start on my vacation early tomorrow morning—before daylight, in fact. I thought I'd go by train for a change and spend a few days in New York looking through art galleries and seeing old friends. I planned to go alone, but it would be so much more fun if you went with me. We'd be real sisters off on a vacation together," Honey finished enthusiastically.

"It sounds wonderful," agreed Judy, "but we won't go by train this time. We'll take turns driving the car. I have a whole week to myself with no house to keep and no cat—"

"No cat!" exclaimed Honey. "Is that a rabbit I see peeking out of Grandma's apron pocket? And that other one sleeping in the box! It looks to me as if you have plenty of cats."

"Kittens," Judy corrected her, laughing.

"They're on their way to becoming cats, aren't they? That's why so many people don't like kittens," Honey said. "They grow up to be cats."

"Good house cats like old Checker," Grandma Dobbs put in defensively, stroking the little calico kitten. "Judy named this one Chessie. Isn't it cute?"

"Adorable!" exclaimed Honey. "They're both adorable. May I hold the little black one? Where did you get them, Judy? Whose kittens are they?"

"They're Blackberry's," Judy said, still laughing, "but he doesn't know it. Helen Brandt's yellow Tabby is the mother. Helen offered me all six of them, but I only took two."

"Won't Blackberry object?"

"I left him with the people who are renting our house," Judy explained briefly. The kittens, she said, were to be given away. Honey was delighted to learn that little Chessie had already found a home with her grandparents.

"We'll take the other one to New York with us, won't we?" she asked. "Is the kitten for Judy Irene, so she'll have a Blackberry, too? I wonder if little Judy will be anything like you when she grows up."

"I don't suppose so. She'll probably be much more sophisticated," Judy said. "She won't be three until November, and already she appears regularly on Irene's Golden Girl show to advertise the sponsor's golden corn cereal. Have you tried it?"

"Once," Honey said, "with strawberries. I don't like cereal without fruit, but I guess I'd eat straw if Irene advertised it. Whenever I see her face on the screen or hear her golden voice I think of the way Lois and Lorraine and all that crowd used to snub her. Now they tell people proudly that Irene Meredith is their friend. It used not to be that way, did it, when she was Irene Lang?"

"It certainly didn't," Judy agreed. "I'll never forget the day Lois warned me that if I made a friend of Irene, none of the downtown girls would have anything to do with me. Farringdon has certainly changed since then." She added with a little sigh, "It seems strange to be here with the house in Dry Brook Hollow rented and my folks not even knowing I'm in Farringdon."

"Doesn't Horace know it?" Honey began. "He said he was going to help you move things."

"He helped us move things all right," Judy told her. "Our personal stuff is all stored in the attic along with the things my grandparents left for me to sort. I'll get around to it some day."

"Of course you will, dear. Don't think about it now," Grandma Dobbs advised brightly. "You just stay here and have supper with us. Then you and Honey can start off on your trip bright and early in the morning."

"You can sleep with me. Remember how we used to stay all night with each other and tell secrets?" Honey asked. "We kept everybody awake whispering."

"You can't do that tonight if you expect to get an early start in the morning," Grandpa Dobbs said firmly. "Take care, now, and don't let Honey drive in traffic. She just got her license and hasn't had much experience yet."

"She will have by the time she comes home," Judy declared. "There's a lot of road between here and New York. We should be there by noon if we start before daylight. That'll mean doing everything this evening. I did plan to stop at the florist's shop. I had him make up a corsage—"

"A corsage? How lovely!" Honey exclaimed. "Was that before you knew your plans would have to be changed?"

"No, it was afterwards."

"If you've ordered flowers you'll have to pick them up before the shop closes. We'll be back in half an hour," Honey said airily as she pulled Judy toward the door.

Judy had left the car parked in front of the apartment building. Honey hurried toward it. Immediately she wanted to drive.

"How did Peter happen to leave the Beetle for you?"

she asked as she slipped behind the wheel. "Won't he need it in Washington? How long can you keep it? I'd like to tour the whole country, but of course we can't do that. You've been so many places, Judy."

"Not too many," Judy replied. "You've been a few places yourself. Remember Thousand Island Camp? And you spent a whole year in New York going to art school, too. I never went away to school at all. Sometimes I wish I had."

"What would you want to study?" Honey asked when they were on their way.

"Oh, the stuff Peter is learning. Not how to shoot, of course. I'm afraid of guns. But I would like to know more about the detection of crime. He was going to show me through the crime lab and explain a lot of things—Oh, here we are," she said, as Honey brought the car to an abrupt stop before the florist shop.

Judy's corsage of snapdragons was ready and waiting for her. Honey took it from its nest of crinkly green paper and pinned it to Judy's suit.

"It certainly looks lovely on you," Honey said.

"That's why I ordered this corsage," Judy confessed. "I thought it would make me feel a little less abandoned, but a corsage is for happy occasions—"

"We'll make this a happy occasion," declared Honey. "You and I are about to set out on a thrilling adventure. Just believe it, Judy, and I'm sure we can make it come true."

CHAPTER V

Turtle Crossing

Judy shook her head.

"That other girl with the corsage probably thought she was about to set out on a thrilling adventure, too," she said, "but what happened? The man she was supposed to meet at the airport never showed up."

"What man?" asked Honey, interested. "Tell me about it."

The story waited until that night when they were in Honey's room packing the things they would need on the trip.

"I've found out that it's always best to take twice as much money as you think you will need, and half as many clothes," declared Judy. "You can always buy things, but if you run out of cash and you're stranded way off in the middle of nowhere—"

"You've had it," Honey finished, laughing. "We won't let that happen to us."

"I don't mean you should take a lot of cash with you. Traveler's checks are safest."

"I have them," said Honey, checking. "I have lots of fresh blouses to wear with my suit, and a good dress that doesn't need ironing. You just rinse it out and hang it up, and it drips dry."

"Good," approved Judy. "I have one, too. They're just the thing when you're traveling light. Is there anything else?"

"The story," Honey reminded her. "You were going to tell me about that man at the airport."

"Well," Judy began, "his name is Charles Nogard. I'm not very likely to forget that, because they kept calling him and calling him over the loudspeaker. Finally the girl got tired of waiting and went away. This Charlie Nogard, whoever he is, was supposed to have come in on that plane Peter took to Washington. It came from Buffalo, I think. The girl was wearing a corsage of snapdragons. I ordered one like it on impulse. Now I wish I hadn't. You haven't any corsage."

"Oh, yes, I do," Honey reassured her. "I have one made out of beads and wires. Forrest Dean's little sister Birdella made it. She's clever that way. When she grows up she may take my place in her father's studio. By then I'll be married—"

"Oh?" Judy said.

She was sitting on the bed watching Honey pack her sketchbook and pencils. Honey closed her suitcase and went over to the mirror to brush her hair. Judy could see her face in the glass. It was thoughtful, preoccupied.

"You have problems, too, don't you?" Judy asked.

"Not in the present," Honey replied. "Only in the future. Maybe I'll be Mrs. Dean when I finally do get married. It would serve Horace just right. He gets me so exasperated—"

"Is that why you're taking this vacation?"

"Frankly, yes. I thought I might meet somebody nicer than either of them," Honey admitted, joining Judy on the bed and becoming confidential. "Forrest ignores me when other girls are around, and Horace is beginning to treat me as if I were his sister, too. I thought, if he had to spend a few evenings by himself . . ."

"I see," Judy said when Honey paused, confused. "But do you think New York is the place to find Prince Charming?"

"Irene found her Prince Charming there. She met Dale Meredith on that bus you girls took to New York. I'll never forget how the rest of us stood there waving good-bye and wishing we could go, too."

"Why didn't you say so, Honey?"

"It would have been impossible. Grandpa and Grandma needed me. I'd been away from them long enough. We had to make up to each other for all the time I didn't know I had any grandparents."

"And for all the time you didn't know Peter was your very own brother," Judy added.

Honey sighed thankfully. "I might not know even yet, if you hadn't been so good at solving mysteries. Judy, can you understand what it was like, suddenly finding a family? You've always been so secure."

"I suppose I have." Judy lay back on the pillows thinking about this. She had never valued security much. It wasn't all she wanted from life. Sometimes she wondered if she really knew what she did want. There were gray days, like the one just ending, and happy ones when she felt that all her wishes would eventually come true. Right now she felt an aching homesickness for the house in Dry Brook Hollow. "Just because it's rented," she told herself.

"What's rented?" asked Honey. Without realizing it, Judy had been speaking aloud.

"Our house," she said. "Remember Ol' Miss Pringle? But, of course, you wouldn't remember her. You weren't living with your grandparents then. She was the librarian in Roulsville before the flood. Now she's married to Robert Wheatley. They are taking care of her brother's little boy. His parents abandoned him."

"They did? Why on earth would they do a terrible thing like that?" Honey asked in amazement.

Judy sighed deeply. "I wish I knew why. I wish I knew a lot of things about them. I don't mean to be suspicious. Peter trusts them, and I guess I should. Renting the house was the sensible thing to do as long as he has to be away so much. In the meantime, Peter said it would be a good idea for us to take a vacation together."

"You and me?" Honey snuggled closer to Judy. "I think it's a good idea, too. We haven't seen enough of each other. Sisters should, you know. I've always wanted a sister."

"You got one when I married Peter," Judy told her affectionately just before they turned out the light. "Don't let me forget my snapdragons in the morning," she added sleepily. "I put them in the refrigerator."

In the morning, the corsage of snapdragons was not forgotten, and neither was the little black kitten. Honey placed him in a basket with a soft flannel to keep him warm. The two girls were up before dawn making themselves ready for the trip. It was a misty morning, and chilly, too. Judy had to wear her white car coat over her suit. Inside the Beetle, with the heater on, she removed it. Driving along with the corsage pinned in place, she discovered that her moods had nothing to do with the weather. It had been sunny and warm the day before when she felt so depressed. Today, in the mist and the rain, she was all sunshine.

"Where shall we go first?" she asked, suddenly aware that the whole country was theirs to explore.

"To Irene's, I guess. We have to deliver this kitten," Honey replied with a fond glance toward the basket she was holding. "I'm sure something exciting will develop. I don't know just what. Plenty of exciting things happened the last time you were in New York."

"Too exciting," Judy agreed. "I wouldn't want to repeat them. City life is not for me. I prefer the wide open spaces."

Honey giggled. Here in the hills of Pennsylvania, the spaces were not so wide. A big truck loomed ahead of them in the mist. Judy had overtaken it on a curve and didn't dare pass until the road widened and gave her more room.

"There!" she announced finally when the truck was far behind. "Now we can really zoom along with nothing in our way."

"Wait!" cried Honey, clutching Judy by the sleeve. "I see something."

"A turtle!" Judy exclaimed, swerving to avoid hitting the slow-moving creature.

"He should wear a sign on his back, TURTLE CROSSING," Honey began, laughing.

Her laughter changed to an exclamation of dismay. Judy had swerved too far. The car careened crazily. In another moment it would be dashed to pieces in the ravine below!

CHAPTER VI

The Mysterious Mr. Nogard

THE highway, at this point, was built along a hill-side with the extreme northern tip of the Blue Ridge mountain range on the left and with the deep gorge of the Susquehanna River far below on the right. Judy had stopped the car in time to keep it from going over, but it was tilted precariously on the edge of the cliff.

Honey took one look and put one hand over her eyes while, with the other hand, she clutched the handle of the kitten's basket. At any other time she might have admired the scenery, but not with the car in this perilous position. The left wheels were still on the cement, but the right wheels had slipped over onto what the road signs had warned them were "soft shoulders." It looked like the end of the poor Beetle. The car tilted more and more as the right wheels settled in the mud.

Judy had to think fast. She opened the door on the left. "Jump," she commanded Honey. "Slide up this way and jump before the whole car turns on its side and rolls into the river."

She reached for Honey's hand and, somehow, she managed to pull her clear. The kitten, jolted out of his sleep, began to mew plaintively. Both girls were shaking like leaves. When Honey could find her voice she said remorsefully, "If I hadn't grabbed your arm, this wouldn't have happened."

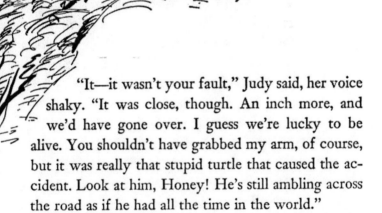

"It—it wasn't your fault," Judy said, her voice shaky. "It was close, though. An inch more, and we'd have gone over. I guess we're lucky to be alive. You shouldn't have grabbed my arm, of course, but it was really that stupid turtle that caused the accident. Look at him, Honey! He's still ambling across the road as if he had all the time in the world."

"I hope he makes it. I hate to see anything killed, even a turtle."

"Me, too," agreed Judy, a shiver passing through her whole body. She couldn't help thinking, "It could have been us."

The two girls who had started out so happily that morning now clung to each other, too badly shaken to try and do anything about the Beetle although the bank looked ready to give way at any moment.

"What'll we do?" Honey asked at last.

"Here comes another car. We'll signal for help," Judy began. Then she saw that there was no need to signal. The green car was already stopping. A perfectly stunning-looking young man leaned out and called in a friendly voice, "In trouble, girls? Is there anything I can do to help?"

"There certainly is," Judy told him gratefully.

As the young man approached them she studied his face more closely. It was fine and thin, and he had a humorous look in his blue eyes and about the corners of his mouth. "Not as strong a face as Peter's," she thought, "but his features are more regular."

In fact, the young man's features were so regular that they made him almost too good-looking. Honey observed this, kitten basket in hand and both eyes wide open in admiration.

"Pinch me!" she whispered. "I must be dreaming. Here comes Prince Charming himself to the rescue."

"Sh!" Judy cautioned her. "He'll hear you."

"What if he does?" Honey returned recklessly. "We need to be rescued, don't we?"

The young man did hear that.

"My word!" he exclaimed, chuckling. "Two damsels in distress. Is that your car tottering at the edge of the cliff?"

"It is," Judy told him. "We were afraid it would

topple over, so we got out. Is there any way to get it back on the road?"

"How did it get off?" His voice was not quite so friendly as it had been at first.

"That!" said Honey pointing to the turtle still only halfway across the highway.

The man took one look and laughed heartily.

"A turtle!" he exclaimed. "Are you soft-hearted or something? You don't have to turn off the road for a turtle. You have the right of way."

"Does the turtle know that?" asked Judy.

This question sent the young man off into another fit of laughter. Observing the kitten in the basket Honey was carrying, he laughed still harder. Judy began to wonder if he had stopped to help them or to be entertained. A cutting question was on the tip of her tongue when another car came along. Fortunately, it was a small truck. Two men in working clothes got out and walked over to the Beetle.

The men from the truck were transporting lumber, and it was soon decided that the best way to get the Beetle back on the road was to place a plank under the right front wheel and then for someone to get in and drive it.

"I'll do it," Judy offered. "It's my car."

The good-looking young man objected to this. "You might see another turtle. It takes a scientific approach—"

The sentence died in his throat as he saw what was there on the seat of the car he was about to drive. It was Judy's corsage still fresh and gay. It almost seemed to her that the flowers were laughing, too. He pointed at them and fairly stammered out his next question.

"You—you were wearing snapdragons?"

"Oh, my corsage!" she exclaimed as he handed her the laughing flowers. "It must have fallen off when I scrambled out of the car. Yes, I was wearing snapdragons. I'd forgotten all about them."

"Were you wearing them yesterday in Farringdon, and were you at the airport?" he asked.

"Why, yes, I—I was," Judy admitted.

"Then who is this girl?" he demanded, turning to Honey. "Why have you brought her with you?"

"She's my sister," Judy retorted. "Why shouldn't I bring her? Look. Are you men going to help us, or shall I walk back to the town we just drove through and telephone the police?"

A look of fear came over the young man's handsome face. "So that's your game? I should have known you were trying to trick me."

"This is no trick," wailed Honey. "Can't you see we need help?"

"Anyone would be a fool to try and move that car. If you want to come with me—"

"We'll help you, lady," one of the other men interrupted. "We'll put planks under the back wheels, too, to make it safe."

They moved off to unload more planks from their truck, and the handsome young man said, "So that's the way you want it?"

"Right now, nothing is the way I want it," Judy replied sharply.

"It's not the way I want it, either," he admitted more politely. "One more question, and I'm through. Was this so-called sister with you yesterday at the airport?"

"No, I was alone——"

"I didn't make the plane," he broke in. "Sorry! You'll forgive me when you see what's in the package."

Thrusting a small paper parcel into Judy's hands, he turned and hurried off to his car.

"Mr. Nogard!" Judy called. She felt sure now that the man would answer to the name she had heard at the airport.

Sure enough, he turned around. But all he said was, "Call me Charlie. Good-bye, Cookie! Hide that package in the basket with the kitten. You hear? There's no change in our plans. I'll see you at the Dragon's Mouth."

Was he joking? Judy stood there bewildered, wondering if he had really said what she thought he said. There was something about the man that was almost unreal.

"What time?" asked Honey as if she were making a date.

"Four o'clock," he called back. "You be there, too. If you're her real sister, it'll be okay with Dan. Remember now, the Dragon's Mouth at four o'clock on Saturday. It's our regular meeting place."

"But I'm not—" Judy began.

Her sentence was lost in the roar of the other motor. Mr. Nogard was off, leaving nothing but the smoke from his exhaust in the place where he had been standing.

CHAPTER VII

A Package of *What?*

A VOICE called Judy out of her bewilderment. It was one of the men from the truck. She looked over to see the Beetle, still tilted precariously, but with planks under the right wheels.

"Well, she's safe now if you're careful. Get in your car, miss, and turn the front wheels as far to the left as you can," the man instructed her as he and his partner stood ready to push. "Don't be afraid now," they told her. "She won't tip over with those planks to guide her. Easy does it."

Automatically, Judy followed their shouted instructions, her mind a confusion of impressions. At last, with a jolt and a bump, the Beetle was back on the road. The turtle, the cause of all the commotion, had crawled off in the bushes and was seen no more.

Honey waited to thank the men. Judy couldn't hear what was said, but it must have been something funny. They went back, laughing, to the task of reloading the muddy planks.

"They were nice, weren't they?" Judy said as Honey climbed into the car with the kitten.

"Dreamy," she agreed, "especially the first one. What happened to him, Judy? Why did he leave so suddenly? I'm beginning to wonder if he was real."

"He wasn't much real help," Judy said in disgust. "He left the men from the truck to do all the work. Handsome is as handsome does, my grandmother used to say. Actually, he didn't do a thing to help get the poor Beetle back on the road. She wasn't damaged at all." Judy laughed. "Now *I'm* doing it. Why do men always talk of ships and cars and motors as if they were girls?"

"They love them, I guess."

"That must be it," agreed Judy. "How do you feel about them, Honey? Would you like to drive?"

"Not—not now," she protested. "I'm afraid, I wouldn't have acted as quickly as you did. Really, Judy, I'm terribly afraid of another accident."

"Well, I'm not," Judy declared, and they were off. "If I drive fast," she continued, "we may overtake

Mr. Nogard and give him back his package. It certainly wasn't intended for us."

"Are you sure?" asked Honey. "He said you'd forgive him when you saw what was in it."

"He didn't mean me. He thought I was that other girl with the corsage, Cookie, or whatever her name is. Probably he was meeting her for the first time. Otherwise he wouldn't have mistaken me for her. A mistake like that could lead to some interesting complications," Judy reflected. "It's happened before. Once I found myself stranded on an Indian Reservation."

"I know," agreed Honey. "That was what I meant when I said you'd been so many places. I meant strange places where exciting things happen."

"I've had enough excitement for one morning right here in Pennsylvania," Judy said with a sigh.

She wished Honey would stop talking for a minute so she could think. The conversation back there by the roadside had been strange enough to suit anybody if she could only recall it. *No change in our plans.* What plans? *It's okay with Dan. The Dragon's Mouth at four o'clock on Saturday.*

"Honey," Judy asked suddenly. "Did you ever hear of a place called The Dragon's Mouth?"

"It sounds like a Chinese restaurant," Honey replied. "Maybe it's in New York. He was headed for New

York, I think. If we don't overtake him, maybe we could find him there. Oh, Judy! Let's do it. Let's find out where The Dragon's Mouth is and be there the way he said. We'll have this package as an excuse—"

"This package of *what?*" Judy interrupted. "It could contain a bomb for all we know. They may be saboteurs plotting to blow up the whole country. They have plans that we know nothing about."

"We could find out about them," Honey suggested.

The package had aroused her curiosity. It was a brown paper bag with the end folded over so that it made a square. A red and white string knotted in the center divided it in four sections. Judy became curious about it, too, but she felt she had no right to open it.

"I'd like to see the contents as much as you would," she admitted to Honey, "but, to tell you the truth, I'm a little afraid of what we might find."

"It must be something nice if you'd forgive him— I mean if Cookie would forgive him for not keeping their appointment," Honey corrected herself.

"If it's something so nice, why did Charlie Nogard tell me to hide it in the kitten's basket?" asked Judy.

Honey giggled. "Maybe it's a catnip mouse." She sniffed the package and then passed it under Judy's nose to see if she detected any odor.

"Please," Judy said, "not while I'm driving. Amuse the kitten with it if you want to. The string's dangling."

Honey lowered the mysterious package back into the basket and the little black kitten, seeing the moving string, pounced on it and caused whatever was inside to crackle.

"It's paper," Honey announced. "Maybe they were pen pals, and that's why they didn't know each other by sight. Maybe they were writing letters to each other, and he saved them for her."

"More likely he saved her letters for no good purpose and then thought better of it and decided to return them. That is," Judy amended her statement, "if they are letters. Money crackles, too."

"Not unless there's an awful lot of it," Honey objected.

Judy laughed. "We're just making a big thing out of nothing," she decided. "The package may contain a simple gift of writing paper. I've seen it in cellophane wrappers that crackle."

"Candy bars are sometimes wrapped in cellophane. Or maybe it's a food package—"

"If it smelled like food I might weaken and open it," confessed Judy. "It's nearly lunchtime. I thought we'd be in New York by noon, but we'll be lucky if we get as far as Scranton. Are you hungry?"

"Starved," Honey said, "but let's not stop for a while. Mr. Nogard may stop. If he's human, he'll get hungry, too."

"What do you mean, 'If he's human'?" asked Judy.

"I keep thinking I may have dreamed him. Real men don't come that handsome. I wonder if he knows how good-looking he is."

"He does if he has a mirror. I still say handsome is—"

"Don't be like Horace—always quoting things. I know I'm being silly. Actually," Honey said, "he paid more attention to you than he did to me."

"Naturally! He thought I was Cookie, his pen pal, or whatever she is."

"Shall I call you Cookie?"

"You may if we meet Charlie Nogard. I would like to give him back his package and find out what's in it or else give it to that girl he thinks he's going to meet at the Dragon's Mouth. He said, 'It's our regular meeting place,' but how could it be if he was meeting this girl, Cookie, for the first time?"

"He was talking about some man named Dan. If it's a double date you can have Dan, or wouldn't Peter approve?" Honey asked teasingly.

Judy had been wondering about Peter herself. Why had he mentioned the word *dragon?* Was it only because of Kevin and his missing Teddy bear and his dinosaur ride? Or could there be a gang who called themselves the dragons? Could the Dragon's Mouth be their meeting place? If so, then this could be her opportunity to help him discover what they were

up to. She glanced over at the package. Honey followed her glance.

"It's a temptation, isn't it?" she asked.

"I'd never open it on purpose, but we couldn't
blame the kitten for tearing a little hole in it, could
we?" Judy asked.

The next time Judy stopped for gas, they both
looked hopefully into the basket. The little black kitten
had lost interest in the package except as a pillow. He
had curled himself around it and fallen asleep. The
package was soft. It crinkled like paper. But its contents remained a mystery.

CHAPTER VIII

A Living Present

JUDY drove fast, trying to make up for lost time, but she did not overtake the car Charlie Nogard was driving. She and Honey both agreed that it must be jet propelled to get so far ahead of them so quickly. At each hilltop they scanned the road ahead, but not a trace of the green convertible did they see. If the man stopped for anything to eat it was not at any of the roadside stands along the way.

"I was right," Honey declared at last. "He isn't human, but I am. Judy, I'm simply famished. We have to buy some milk for the kitten, anyway. He's eaten all the cat food in the basket."

"I was hoping he'd eat a hole in the package. Ah,

well!" Judy said, laughing. "Even if he did, my conscience might tell me not to peek. That's what I get for being Dr. Bolton's daughter. Conscience, to him, is just as real as the stomach or any other organ in the body. We were taught that hunger pangs and conscience pangs were both genuine. Peter was brought up the same way."

"I wish I had been." Every now and then Honey would look back wistfully on the childhood she might have had if her grandparents had known she existed. She rarely talked about her real childhood in the slums of New York. Instead, she talked happily of her year in art school and the friends she had made, or of Irene and the theatrical world. "I went with you to New York in spirit the last time you were there," she reminded Judy. "It must have been thrilling to see behind the scenes in that old theater Irene used as a television studio for her Golden Girl show."

"Scary was the word for it," declared Judy. "I was tempted to believe I really had a phantom friend."

Both Judy and Honey found it easy to make real friends. Irene was one of them. In spite of objections from their schoolmates, they had included her in their circle of friends when she lived on the wrong side of Farringdon's old dividing line and went to high school with them. Now, as the wife of the detective story writer, Dale Meredith, and the mother of little Judy Irene, she was still a friend. Honey had visited the

Merediths in Tower House, but she had never seen the family's new home on Long Island.

"How much farther is it?" she asked Judy as they left the restaurant where they had stopped for a late lunch. Refreshed with hamburgers, cokes, and milk for the kitten, they were ready to be on their way again.

"It will take us about two hours if we don't run into any more trouble," replied Judy, starting the car.

It had been foggy and wet when they left Farringdon that morning, but now the rain seemed to be over. The sun was shining when they reached the flat lands of New Jersey. Traffic became more congested. Suddenly Judy realized how tired she was, but she couldn't ask Honey to drive into the city. They crossed the Hudson River on the George Washington bridge and found their way through the Bronx with very little difficulty. Signs pointed to another bridge over the East River. At last, without driving through downtown New York at all, they crossed to Long Island. Judy consulted her wrist watch.

"Three o'clock," she announced. "Not bad, considering what almost happened to us. Does Irene know we're coming? She expected you, but what about me?"

Honey laughed. "I thought I'd keep you and the kitten for a surprise."

Judy hoped it would be a pleasant surprise. Not everyone liked black cats.

"What'll we do if the kitten isn't welcome?" Judy asked.

"If I know Irene, any gift from you will be welcome," Honey declared warmly.

They were driving along one of Long Island's beautiful parkways. Judy remembered the turn down Grand Avenue. Soon they passed the school little Judy would be attending when she was old enough, turned again, and finally brought the car to a stop before a house at the very end of a street called Brookwold Avenue.

The house was low and rambling with shrubs in front and the green lawn sloping toward the brook that divided this village from the next one. Both were in the township of Hempstead, but each little Long Island village, as Irene had once said, possessed its own character.

"There she is!"

Honey was first to see the door fly open. A graceful fair-haired girl who looked too young to be the mother of the pixie-like child beside her fairly crushed both girls in a double embrace.

"Mommy! Mommy!" cried little Judy as she tried to find a place for herself in the tangle of welcoming embraces. Failing, she turned and shouted toward the house, "Daddy! Come out! Big Doody came back."

Dale Meredith, tall, dark, and handsome as ever, came at his small daughter's command and joined in the general welcome.

"Hug me, too, Doody! Hug me harder!" the baby squealed as Judy picked her up and gave her a tremendous hug.

"Look what Judy's brought for you," Honey said, showing her the kitten's basket and laughing as she plopped down on the grass to examine its contents.

"Oh, Irene, I meant to ask you—" Judy began. But whatever she meant to ask, it was too late. Little Judy had pulled the kitten from the basket and now had it in her arms.

Inside the house she still refused to give up her treasure. She ran to get her doll clothes and began trying to squeeze the kitten into one of the little dresses. Then she squashed a bonnet over its ears and began whirling it around and singing the same words over and over in her excitement.

"It's alive! It's alive! It's alive!" she sang out, hugging the kitten so hard that Judy had to remind her it wouldn't be alive much longer if she didn't give it a chance to breathe.

"I just thought of a song about a little girl who wanted a real live kitten and promised to take good care of it. Shall I sing it for you?" Irene asked to quiet the excited child.

She picked Judy's little namesake up in her arms,
kitten and all, and began to sing softly, each golden
note as pure and true as if she were singing for her
television audience:

"If I had a real live kitty
I would gently smooth its fur.
I would pet it. I would feed it.
I would listen to it purr.
But I still would dress my dollies
In the clothes they like to wear
And not put them on my kitty.
And I'd hug my Teddy bear!"

"Oh, thank you, Mommy!" cried little Judy, drop-
ping the kitten in its ridiculous doll clothes and running
to get her Teddy bear. The kitten seemed to consider
it a substitute for the mother cat and was soon curled
up beside it in the doll carriage. The Teddy bear made
Judy think of something else.

"We rented our house in Dry Brook Hollow to a
Mr. and Mrs. Wheatley," she said. "They've taken
her brother's little boy to bring up because his parents
abandoned him."

"How old is the boy?" Dale asked, immediately
interested in Judy's story.

"About six, I think. Little Judy's Teddy bear made
me think of him. He says a bad man stole his Teddy
bear, but nobody will believe him. I don't know

whether it was lost or stolen, but I do know he misses it. I left Blackberry with him to take the Teddy bear's place."

"Judy, you didn't!" Irene exclaimed. "I didn't think you'd ever give up Blackberry—"

"I'm not giving him up. Kevin just borrowed him," Judy said.

That evening after dinner they talked and talked. Whatever Judy forgot to tell, Honey filled in. Her description of Mr. Nogard was especially detailed. Not satisfied with it, she sketched a picture of him and showed it to Dale and Irene while Judy told them about the turtle episode.

"So the old boy finally made it? I can feel for that turtle," declared Dale. "He's lucky the man in the green convertible stopped in time. What did you say his name was?"

"Nogard. It's an odd name," Honey said thoughtfully. "How would you spell it, Judy? I'll write it under the picture."

"N-O-G-A-R-D, I guess. Honey!" Judy exclaimed, her gray eyes widening in astonishment as she saw the name all written out. In a flash she saw something else. "I don't think your Mr. Nogard would be so handsome," she said, "if you drew a picture of him with his name spelled backwards!"

CHAPTER IX

A Strange Appointment

"Why, what do you mean?" gasped Honey. She glanced at the likeness she had drawn of the mysterious Mr. Nogard with his name underneath in bold letters. Then she saw it, too, and her hand began to work quickly sketching something that faintly resembled a toad.

"Do dragons wear their eyes on the top of their heads?" asked Judy, watching.

Honey giggled. "I never had one for a model, but this will do. There you have him—Mr. Dragon, and we were supposed to meet him at the Dragon's Mouth."

Irene stood up and leaned over the table to see what

Honey was drawing. "What is it?" she asked her. "Why have you drawn that horrible creature beside the handsome Mr. Nogard?"

"Can't you see? It's a dragon. NOGARD spelled backwards reads DRAGON—"

"So it does!" Dale exclaimed. "So that's what you were drawing? I've heard of the reluctant dragon, but this one looks a little too reluctant. Aren't dragons supposed to breathe fire?"

Honey made a few scribbles near the creature's open mouth. "There! Is that better?"

"What about ridges?" asked Judy. "Don't dragons have something that looks like the edge of a pie crust along their backs?"

"Really," Honey said, laughing as she drew a wavy line parallel with the dragon's long neck, "I might as well be back at the studio working for Mr. Dean. He isn't as critical of my drawing as you are."

"Nobody has criticized your drawing of Mr. Nogard," Irene reminded her. "He is handsome. What secret do you suppose he's hiding?"

"I wish I knew! Judy, what do you think all this means?" Honey asked. "Is Nogard a made-up name and not his real name at all?"

"Probably," she agreed, "but that doesn't necessarily mean a great deal. Didn't you ever spell things backwards just for fun?"

"Of course. We spelled *rail* backwards and laughed

our heads off when Horace's parrot shrieked it right out—"

"That's what I mean," Judy continued. "Mr. Nogard probably took that name for fun, too, in the beginning. But if it's letters in that package—"

"What package?" asked Irene, overcome with curiosity.

"It's still in the kitten's basket if little Judy didn't see it and open it—"

"She didn't," Judy interrupted, holding the package aloft. The string was tangled and chewed, but the brown paper bag was unbroken. There was still no way of guessing what might be inside.

"We can't open it," Honey explained. "It belongs to Cookie."

"Is that the kitten's name?" Irene asked innocently.

Judy and Honey began to laugh. They had told Dale and Irene all about the turtle but had forgotten to mention Cookie.

"It's the name of a girl Mr. Nogard was to have met," Judy started to explain, "but he's never seen her, and I was wearing snapdragons—"

"That's how he got them mixed up," Honey put in.

Irene sighed deeply. "You're both mixing me up. How do you two girls happen to have Cookie's package, and what are you going to do with it?"

"We're going to give it to her if we can find her.

That's what we were trying to tell you," Judy said. "Mr. Nogard mistook me for Cookie because I was wearing this corsage. It's a little withered now, but the flowers are snapdragons. He made an appointment with us at a place called the Dragon's Mouth. Do you know where that is?"

"Not offhand," Dale said. Judy had turned to him for an answer. "I could look it up, of course. There are plenty of reference books in my study. Is the place in New York State?"

"That's what we don't know. Honey thought it might be a Chinese restaurant. If it is, we could look it up in the telephone book."

Judy was soon following her own suggestion. But no such Chinese restaurant was listed. The dictionary failed to provide a clue. Dale turned to his travel books, searching through the indexes. Finally he found it. He turned to Judy and Honey, shaking his head.

"I don't think you're going to keep that appointment," he told them. "There's only one Dragon's Mouth listed in this guide book, and it's in Yellowstone National Park."

"Yellowstone!" Judy exclaimed. "Oh, Honey!"

They looked at each other a moment. Their eyes were saying the same thing: *"Let's go there!"*

"How far is it?" Honey asked. "How long will it take us to drive? We'll take turns, of course, so neither of us will get too tired."

"Do you mean you're actually thinking of going there?" Irene asked.

"Why not? This is my vacation. Judy and I have no other plans. If we start early tomorrow morning—that's Wednesday—we could be there by Saturday. Let's get a map and plan the route we'll take," Honey suggested.

"Wait a minute!" All this was a little too sudden even for Judy. "We can't go dashing across the country like that without letting anybody know. Peter gave me a number where he can be reached day or night, and I think I'll call him right now. If he says it's all right I might consider it. After all, the Beetle is his car and he may need it before we'd have time to drive it all the way back."

It was good to hear Peter's voice over the telephone. He had been worried about Judy, he said, and was glad to hear that she and Honey were taking their vacation together.

"I'm afraid I wouldn't see much of you, anyway, if you came to Washington right now. This is a stiff course," he told her. "Go ahead, have yourselves a wonderful time, but keep in touch. I want a letter or a postcard every day. Promise?"

"I promise." That, thought Judy, would be an easy promise to keep.

"Won't you need the Beetle?" she asked. "We thought of driving to—to Yellowstone. We'd stop at tourist places along the way and really see the country."

"You have it all planned, don't you?" Peter asked. "I won't need the car. Go ahead, Angel, but," he added seriously, "drive carefully."

"I will," Judy promised. Suddenly she wanted to cry. Was she afraid? A few inches on the map were, in reality, a great many weary miles of driving. But, with Honey willing to relieve her, it might be possible.

At the table everybody was poring over a road map of the whole United States. They were discussing this route and that route, calling all the roads by numbers as if a trip like this would be as simple as a problem in arithmetic. Honey looked up as Judy returned from making her telephone call.

"What did Peter say? Is it all right?" she asked.

"He didn't object, if that's what you mean."

"Then it's all settled! We are going, aren't we, Judy? Did he say you could have the car?"

"Yes, but—"

Honey wouldn't let her finish. She was whirling her around the room in her excitement, her words tumbling over each other.

"We'll start before daylight and drive as far as Buffalo tomorrow. Maybe we'll cross over and stay in one of those tourist places on the Canadian side. We might even drive as far as Muskegon—"

"Where?" gasped Judy.

"Muskegon, Michigan. Look!" Honey pointed out, showing her the map. "That dotted line means there's a ferry across Lake Michigan. A nice long boat ride will give us a rest from driving."

"We'll need it," declared Judy. "I give in. I can see you have the trip all planned. Where do we go from Muskegon?"

"To Milwaukee," Dale said, "and from there you pick up route sixteen and move straight across the map. It's a scenic route. You take in the Badlands and Mt. Rushmore."

"Is that the mountain with the faces of our Presidents carved on it? I would like to see it," Judy admitted. "I just need a minute to catch my breath and think. We've only been here a few hours."

"We'll understand if you want to cut your visit short," Irene began.

"It isn't that," Judy told her. "I know we'll be welcome the next time we come to New York. It's the purpose of this trip that worries me. Are we really going three-quarters of the way across the country just to return a package that may contain nothing but writing paper? Suppose we can't find the Dragon's Mouth or it isn't the right place? What is it, anyway, a cave or something?"

"Didn't I tell you?" Dale opened the guide book. "Here's a photograph of it. You see, Nature carved the face of a dragon on another mountain. It's a real fire-breathing dragon, too. It says here that every few seconds bursts of steam issue from its throat."

"Is it—dangerous?" Judy was thinking back to something Mrs. Wheatley had said about the hot springs in Yellowstone. But the picture reassured her. Groups of tourists were standing around an innocent-appearing crater watching a vapor-like mist that looked no more deadly than a summer cloud.

CHAPTER X

Apprehensions

"So THIS is a real fire-breathing dragon? I'll have to see it to believe it," declared Judy, studying the guidebook. "Don't let me forget my camera. I'm sure I can take a better picture than this. Let's compare it with that dragon you drew, Honey. The one in the guidebook has a much longer nose."

"His mouth is wide open, too. My poor little dragon looks sick next to this one. Oh, Judy! I can hardly wait to sketch the real one," Honey burst out enthusiastically. "I wish we had more time to take pictures and sketch things along the way."

"There may be a little time if we start early and drive all day tomorrow," Judy said.

"Take the thruway to Buffalo," Dale suggested. "I've marked the most direct route with a red pencil. It takes you straight across the map. Keep my highway atlas as a guide and you won't get lost."

"You'll need a good night's rest. The guest room is ready," Irene announced.

"Thanks, Irene," Judy replied. "Good night, both of you. Will little Judy be up to see us off?"

"She arises with the birds," declared Dale. "I think she'll be up especially early tomorrow morning because of the kitten. She's been calling it Blackie. That could be short for Blackberry. Do you mind?"

"You don't like the name Blackie, do you?" Irene asked when Judy hesitated.

"It brings back unpleasant memories," Judy confessed. "I knew a criminal who called himself Blackie. How about Jet Blackberry? Then little Judy could call the kitten Jettie for short."

Dale and Irene agreed. Apparently, little Judy did, too. They must have suggested the name to her when she was half asleep. Just as Dale had predicted, she was up with the birds and so was the kitten. She made it wave its paw when Judy and Honey were ready to leave. The last thing they heard as they drove away was little Judy's "Thank you for Dettie!"

"She'll be able to pronounce her J's the next time we see her," Judy predicted.

"Dale thinks we can drive all the way to Yellowstone by Saturday," Honey said, "but if anything happens—"

"What, for instance?"

"Another turtle."

"He wouldn't stand a chance," declared Judy. "We'll soon be on the thruway, and you'll see. Cars go awfully fast."

Judy was not used to driving at such speed, but soon found it exhilarating. The atlas had taken the kitten's place. Honey divided her attention between the maps in it and the passing scenery. Not much was said as both girls were intent on covering as many miles as possible that first day of driving. It was Wednesday, still early in the week.

"He said four o'clock on Saturday, didn't he? That gives us four full days of driving. Let's see." Honey took a tape measure from her tote bag and began measuring the distance on the big map of the United States inside the cover of the opened atlas. "It's exactly eighteen inches to Yellowstone. If one inch equals one hundred miles that means we have eighteen hundred miles to cover. Divide that by four and we have to drive four hundred and fifty miles a day."

"It would be easy if we had roads like this all the way. Isn't there a mileage chart on the back of that atlas Dale gave us?" asked Judy. "Your tape measure doesn't allow for all the little twists and turns. I think it's more than eighteen hundred miles."

Honey consulted the chart. "Oh dear! You're right, Judy," she admitted. "The chart says it's over two thousand miles. That means five hundred miles a day. It won't be so easy, will it?"

"It will be downright impossible," Judy told her. "Maybe we ought to give up the whole idea."

"Oh, please!" begged Honey. "You've done the impossible before. You know you have, Judy. This time let's do it together."

"Well," Judy conceded, "we have covered three hundred miles in less than five hours. If you'll take your turn at the next gas station and let me see the map, I'll try and figure out how many inches we have to go before we stop for a rest. We can't overdo it."

Thinking of the distance in inches made the long trip ahead of them seem shorter. Although Honey was not used to driving at high speed, she handled the car like an expert. They were ready to leave the thruway and cross Niagara Bridge by noon.

"Can't we stop and see the falls?" she asked. "I've never seen them."

"I'll drive, and you can look at them while we're crossing," Judy replied impatiently. She didn't want to stop. She wanted to keep the memory of the day Peter had surprised her with the rainbows and they had told each other they stood for unexpected happiness.

The unexpected had happened, but it had not always

been happy. Peter's job was a dangerous one. Twice he had been seriously hurt and once nearly killed in a landslide. Would there be dangers like that on the road ahead? Judy began to feel apprehensive.

"Oh!" exclaimed Honey as they crossed. She had seen the rainbows, too. The beauty of Niagara seen through a rainbow mist left her breathless. "It was so beautiful, and we went by so quickly—"

"We'll stop on this side for lunch and feast on scenery as well as sandwiches," Judy decided when they were in Canada. She found a familiar restaurant where she and Peter had lunched on their honeymoon. Cards and souvenirs were for sale at a counter near the window. A table was placed nearby. Honey was still finishing her lunch when Judy thought of something.

"I'll buy one of those postcards and send it right away. I promised Peter I'd write every day," she said as she excused herself from the table.

On the picture postcard she wrote one word, "Remember?" and stood at the window lost in dreams.

"Hurry up, Judy," she heard Honey's voice at her elbow. "Tell him everything's fine, and let's be on our way. I've just figured it out. We went four inches this morning. If we go four more this afternoon we'll be at Muskegon, and that's where we get the ferry. We can sleep on the boat."

"Four inches! Oh, Honey! This car isn't a real beetle

crawling along the map. We can't crawl. We'll have to drive like crazy to make it, and I'm not sure I want to."

"I do. I'll drive." Eagerly Honey slid behind the wheel and headed the car west. Judy had to make her slow down a little. This wasn't the thruway. A ticket for speeding would surely make them lose their race for the boat.

"What time does it leave?" Judy asked. "Does it say on the map?"

"I didn't see any time. Didn't Dale say there was a night boat? We'll be there by night. This route misses all the big cities except Grand Rapids."

"What about Flint?" Judy was looking at the map of Michigan. "We go right through the center of it. There may be traffic."

Honey didn't think so. She kept on driving until late that afternoon. The route they were taking crossed Canada north of Lake Erie and finally brought them into a city called Sarnia. Judy had never heard of it before, but it appeared to be quite a busy metropolis. Traffic lights and a toll bridge slowed them down. The bridge took them across the extreme southern end of Lake Huron and back into the United States.

"Home again!" breathed Honey. "It's your turn to drive after we grab a bite to eat."

"Do you still think we can catch that boat? I don't," declared Judy. "I don't see how we can be in Muskegon before midnight unless the Beetle sprouts wings."

"Let's hope it's a midnight boat—"

"It may not be running at all this early in the season. April weather is changeable—"

"May weather," Honey corrected her. "Everything opens up the first of May. It says so on the map." She pointed to a little square marked *U. S. National Parks*. "It says, under Yellowstone, '*Limited accommodations May first to June nineteenth and from September fifteenth to snow.*'"

Judy shivered. "I hadn't thought of snow. It will be cold in Yellowstone this time of year. How limited are their accommodations? I hope there's heat in the cabins or wherever it is we're going to stay. It will be cold on the boat, too."

Honey didn't seem to mind. "We brought our warm coats," she responded cheerfully.

CHAPTER XI

Where Dinosaurs Roamed

"WHAT's the matter, Judy?" Honey asked after another hundred miles, or what she called an inch of driving.

"Oh, nothing," Judy replied. "If I look worried it's just because I was thinking what a joke it would be on us if we drove all this way and forgot that package."

"Judy, you didn't—"

"Calm down. It's in my suitcase."

"Are you sure?"

"Well, pretty sure," Judy replied. "We'll look the next time we stop. Now relax and enjoy the scenery while you can. It will soon be dark."

They drove on and on through the darkness. Judy wasn't sleepy, but her arms were beginning to ache. She glanced at Honey sound asleep beside her and thought how foolish they both were not to stop and sleep more comfortably in one of the many motels along the way.

All the movie houses were closed by the time they reached Grand Rapids. The city was dark except for the street lights. Judy saw a sign with the number 16 on it and knew they had found their road. Automatically she turned. Honey slept on to be awakened an hour later by the shrill sound of a boat whistle.

"We made it!" Judy announced triumphantly. "It's a one-o'clock boat."

She was glad to let an attendant drive the Beetle down the ramp. The boat started almost at once. Judy could hear the motor and the soft swish of waves against its sides.

"It just moves," Honey said dreamily. "We don't have to do a thing about it."

Above, in the luxurious lobby, Judy sank down on a sofa and closed her eyes. Never again, she resolved, would she drive so many miles in a single day. On the map it was only a little more than seven inches, but she knew now how deceptive a map can be.

"I hope you're not too tired to open your suitcase and see if that package is there," Honey said presently.

"You open it. Here's the key."

Judy thrust it into Honey's hands. The package, its mysterious contents intact, was right on top of Judy's folded clothing. She selected a fresh blouse for morning and was about to close the suitcase when Honey said, "We won't be carrying our suitcases when we meet Mr. Nogard. Will it be all right if I keep the package in my tote bag?"

"As you like," sighed Judy, too tired to care.

She remembered nothing of the boat ride. Morning came and with it an awareness of other passengers preparing to leave.

"Come on, Judy. This is Milwaukee," Honey urged her. "We start driving again."

"So soon?" She gathered her things together and joined the other passengers. The Beetle was waiting. Judy fancied the car looked a little rested, too. Or was it only because the attendant had given it such good care on the boat? She gave him a generous tip, and they were off again, driving fifty miles before they stopped for breakfast at a little lake resort.

Wisconsin was dotted with lakes. Everything was green except for whole fields of yellow flowers. As they drove, the farms began to thin out. There were long stretches of cool, green forests that made Judy homesick for her own grove in Dry Brook Hollow.

"It's too quiet, too peaceful," she thought with something very close to a premonition of disaster. She remembered that Kevin had started for Yellow-

The mysterious package was there

stone too, but had never arrived. Judy wished now that she had paid more attention to his problem. Peter had listened very patiently when the little boy had chattered about how good his father and mother were. And yet they had abandoned him. "Why?" Judy wondered. It seemed especially cruel right after promising him he could see the bears in Yellowstone.

"Honey," Judy asked, "do you think we will see any bears?"

"We haven't seen anything but rabbits so far," Honey replied, "but look! There's a new kind of animal. He just popped up beside the road. Did you see him?"

"There's another!" exclaimed Judy. "Aren't they cute? I think they must be prairie dogs."

"Are we on the prairie?"

"We will be soon." Judy consulted the map. She was holding it now, and Honey was driving. "Route sixteen is just north of the state line between Minnesota and Iowa. That's prairie. See how flat everything is."

"It's rather monotonous, isn't it? I liked Wisconsin better."

"Shall we go back?"

"After coming this far? Not on your life," Honey said with a laugh. "We did the impossible yesterday. If we drive all day today we can take time to enjoy ourselves tomorrow."

By eight o'clock that evening both girls were ready for a rest. Taking turns at the wheel, they had moved the Beetle another four inches along the map. They lost a little time when they drove off the main highway to visit Mystery Cave in Minnesota, but soon made it up. Now they were in South Dakota, and Judy was sitting at a desk in her comfortable motel room telling Peter about the trip.

"We've had good roads all the way," she wrote, "except when we took a side road to see Mystery Cave. I wish you could have explored it with us. The rocky walls were all colors of the rainbow, and the lake inside was the bluest blue I have ever seen. It looked shallow because it was so still, but it was really deep. The guide lowered a pole to show us. Then he took us into a high part of the cave that reminded me of our own cathedral rock at home. That was all the sightseeing we did today. Tomorrow we'll see the Badlands and Mt. Rushmore, and the next day we'll be in Yellowstone . . ."

Judy paused in her writing. Would it be that easy? She told Peter nothing of her apprehensions and even forgot to mention the package they had come so far to return. She had almost forgotten it when, suddenly, the next day, a car shot past them and Honey screamed with more urgency than good grammar:

"Look, Judy! It's *him*. That's Mr. Nogard in the green car. He just passed us. Please drive a little faster. Maybe we can overtake him."

Judy drove as fast as she dared. The view on either

side of the road reminded her of Westerns she had seen on television—the bare, rocky ground with clumps of sagebrush and strange, grass-covered buttes.

"We should be Indians chasing him on horseback. I think we're coming into the Badlands. I don't want to speed along here," Judy said at last. "We'll see him in Yellowstone anyway, and I did want to take some time to explore. Wouldn't you like to stand on one of those buttes and pretend we're in prehistoric times when dinosaurs roamed over this part of America?"

"Did they?" asked Honey. "I can believe it. How strange and different everything is! I would like to explore those weird rock formations up ahead. We have time to take a few pictures."

Time was almost forgotten as the girls photographed each other climbing in and out among the purple rocks. Some were shaped like toadstools. Others reached over like clutching hands. These were more of a shell pink. Great sections of land had fallen away, leaving ridges that looked like the ramparts of giant castles.

"Maybe we can find a mastodon bone or something. Doesn't it scare you to think that this was the work of Nature?" asked Honey, poking about among the crumbling rocks.

"Let's go," Judy said at last. "I want to take a picture of Mt. Rushmore before it gets dark. We have to drive through Rapid City—"

"Let's keep on pretending until we get there, shall

we?" Honey suggested as she took the wheel. It was her turn to drive, but the Beetle was no longer a car, she declared. A car seemed out of place in this ancient setting. It was a dinosaur.

"What kind?" asked Judy. "There are several kinds, you know. I know a funny verse about one kind that begins:

> *"Behold the armored Dinosaur*
> *With a face no mother could adore.*
> *He had a mien that was very solemn*
> *And a most peculiar spinal column."*

"What was it like?" asked Honey, giggling. "His spinal column, I mean."

"Oh, sort of up and down—"

"Like those sand hills we passed?"

"More like that dragon you drew. He was called a stegosaurus," Judy added, "and there were others with even more unpronounceable names. The fierce tyrannosaurus and a milder creature with a long neck and tail—"

"Like that one up ahead?" Honey's voice was suddenly amazed and incredulous. "Oh, Judy! We pretended too hard," she declared as she drove nearer the hill that loomed up beyond Rapid City. "Now we're seeing real dinosaurs!"

CHAPTER XII

Carved in Stone

Rapid City, Judy remembered as they drove through it, had been the scene of an armed bank robbery the previous September. It looked quiet enough now. Even the "dinosaurs" were quiet. They were to be seen on a sloping green hill beyond the city.

"That one," said Judy, as if it were nothing unusual to encounter half a dozen prehistoric monsters on an afternoon's drive, "is called the brontosaurus. He was the largest—"

"*Was?*" Honey exclaimed. "You mean he *is*. Those things are supposed to be extinct."

"And so," Judy continued, enjoying Honey's bewilderment, "someone carved full-size statues of them

82

and placed them in a park. I suspected as much when Kevin said his daddy had let him ride on a dinosaur."

"It could have been one of those!"

"Exactly," agreed Judy. "To tell you the truth, I knew they'd be there. You see, I bought a giant-size postcard when we stopped for lunch. It shows a picture of that hill up ahead. I thought we'd visit Dinosaur Park—"

"Is that its name? Why doesn't someone tell me these things?" asked Honey. "That brontosaurus gave me the scare of my life. It's a wonder I didn't wreck the car."

Judy laughed. "You were in perfect control. Anyway, I thought we'd visit Dinosaur Park and explore the possibilities of dinosaur riding ourselves and then I'd tell Peter all about it on the picture postcard. He's interested in Kevin, and if I can find out just a little, it may help."

"Don't tell him how those dinosaurs scared me."

"I won't," Judy promised. "Now shall we park the car and climb those steps up to the park? I'd like to take a picture of you sitting on a dinosaur. You could send it to Horace to keep in his wallet. I can just imagine him taking it out to look at it."

"Look at what?" Honey demanded, "Me or the dinosaur? If I know that brother of yours, he'd be more interested in the dinosaur than he would be in me." She stopped near the top of the steps, eyeing the creature. "He does have a most peculiar spinal column, doesn't he? Those ruffles on his back will make him easy to climb."

Honey climbed up and soon was sitting comfortably between his "ruffles."

"All set for the dinosaur ride," she called out. "Do you think this will make a good picture?"

"Excellent," agreed Judy, looking into her camera. "From this angle I get you and the dinosaur as well as a good view of Rapid City. I can even see the bank. I hoped we'd be here before it closed so I could cash another traveler's check."

"You can cash them anywhere," Honey said just as Judy snapped the picture.

"This bank was a little special." She climbed up to sit beside Honey on the dinosaur's back. "Now I can tell you about it," she began. "Did you know it was robbed last September? Kevin's dinosaur story places his parents in Rapid City the very day it was robbed. He was abandoned the next day. Anyway, that's what the Wheatleys believe. I think there's more to the story than that, don't you?"

"What do you mean?" asked Honey. "Investigating a bank robbery is a job for the police or the FBI. People who rob banks are dangerous—"

"I know that," Judy interrupted. "That's why I can't believe the Pringles had anything to do with it. The

Wheatleys are a little too eager to think the worst of them."

"Well, if they abandoned Kevin, what can anybody think?"

"But why? Why? That's what I want to find out. Why did they do it? He loved them, and they must have loved him. I knew Peggy Pringle. She did like pretty clothes, but what girl doesn't? And I can't believe they could be more important to her than her own little boy. And what about his father? A man who would bring his son up here to play one day wouldn't go off and leave him alone in a tourist cabin the next."

"Is that what they did? Where is the tourist cabin?" Honey asked.

"I wish I knew. They said somewhere in the Black Hills, and they're just west of here. Mt. Rushmore is one of the peaks. Let's go back to the car and look at the map," Judy suggested.

Honey seemed reluctant to leave the dinosaurs.

"Didn't you say Peter called them land dragons?" she asked, looking back at them a little wistfully as she and Judy descended the long steps.

They found the atlas on the car seat right where they had left it. The giant post card Judy intended to send Peter marked the map of South Dakota with route sixteen turning southwest at Rapid City and branching at a place called Keystone. Here it was crossed by a little blue road that, apparently, rejoined route sixteen.

"It's sort of a short cut, isn't it?" asked Honey. "It takes us right past Mt. Rushmore National Monument. Let's stop and see the Presidents and then drive on to the next tourist place. It just might be the one. We've been lucky so far."

"Except for the turtle," Judy reminded her.

"Oh, that was luck, too. If it hadn't been for the turtle we wouldn't have met Mr. Nogard, and if we hadn't met him," Honey continued, "we wouldn't be on our way to Yellowstone to return his package. I'm glad we saw him again, aren't you? At least we know he's going to be there tomorrow."

"It is tomorrow, isn't it? We'll be there," Judy said with confidence. "It's only another three inches."

"But that big map fools you," Honey pointed out. "I don't think we ought to waste any time. If we really want to keep that date at the Dragon's Mouth we should be at least a third of the way across Wyoming before we stop."

"You're right, Honey." Judy was driving now. The afternoon was almost gone when they reached Mt. Rushmore. It was every bit as magnificent as Judy had hoped it would be. She and Honey climbed up to the observation platform of the building just opposite and gazed across at the great memorial mountain.

There were the heads of the Presidents just as Judy had seen them in pictures. But seeing them in reality was different, somehow. It made her proud of Peter and the work he was doing for the government.

"They're so big!" exclaimed Honey, catching hold of Judy's arm and pulling her over to the rail. The mountain dropped straight down into a gorge below.

"They were big—big in every way," declared Judy, naming the Presidents in the order that the sculptor had carved them. "George Washington, the father of our country, and Thomas Jefferson, who visioned a true democracy. I always think of Teddy Roosevelt as the President who inspired the Teddy bear, but he did more than that. And then there was Lincoln—"

"We're still trying to live up to his ideals," Honey put in, and the two girls were silent, feeling more than they could express in words. Finally the spell was broken when another spectator, one of a group of boys, pointed to the fallen chips of granite beneath the opposite mountain and said, "Look at all that rock down there. It must have been some job to chisel it away. I wonder what he got out of it."

"Who?" his companion asked.

"That fellow, Borglum. You know, the sculptor who carved those faces."

"I don't know." The other shrugged. "They say he died before he finished it. Some people work themselves to death, and others get money without working. Take that bank job last fall as an example. I was there when that guy pulled it. He just whips a handkerchief out of his pocket, covers his pretty face, walks up to the window, hands the girl a paper bag and she dumps in the money. It was as easy as that. She didn't start yelling for the cops until he was out of the bank."

"Honey, did you hear that?" Judy whispered excitedly. "That's just the way the Farringdon bank was robbed!"

"If we can get a description of that bank robber—" Honey began.

"The boy saw his face," Judy said. "Wait a minute!"

Judy's call stopped the group of students. They were only schoolboys trying to act tough.

"Yeah? What is it?"

"That bank robber you saw. Can you describe him?"

"Well, he was a good-looking guy—"

"What are you, crazy or something?" his companion stopped him. "Mr. Jaret is waiting. You want to get us in trouble talking with strangers?"

CHAPTER XIII

Lost in the Black Hills

THE words the boys had spoken seemed to echo back from the mountain opposite as they hurried off with their teacher.

"We're strangers to them. They wouldn't talk with us," Honey said, looking at Judy in disbelief.

"I know. I guess I asked for it," Judy admitted. "The other day, Horace referred to something from a modern psalmist. I can't remember it, but it was about his vision of a righteous nation, and he said there were no strangers under the heavens."

"That's a beautiful thought," Honey said softly. "It's from *Psalms of the West*, one of Horace's favorite sources. It was like him to quote it."

"I was calling the Wheatleys strangers. It does seem strange that they're living in our house and that her brother is suspected of robbing a bank way out here. He isn't good looking," Judy continued. "In fact, he's almost as unattractive as she is, only that kind of a face doesn't look so out of place on a man. The little boy is more like his mother. I used to admire Peggy Pringle and wish I had beautiful blond hair like hers."

"You and your hair!" Honey scolded. "Lots of people would give their eyeteeth to be glamorous redheads."

"Name one." Judy was not feeling very glamorous. She shivered. "It's cold out here. Even the Presidents look cold. Let's go inside and have hot coffee and something to eat."

Buffaloburgers were being served in the restaurant. Judy and Honey sat where they could still look out on Mt. Rushmore and sampled them.

"They taste almost like beef," Honey said when she had taken a bite. "It seems a shame to eat buffalo, doesn't it? I thought they were nearly extinct."

"Aren't you thinking of dinosaurs?"

"I wonder if we'll see any. I mean buffalo, of course," Honey corrected herself, laughing.

"There are supposed to be great herds of them in Yellowstone." Judy walked over to a rack where she chose several postcards. "See this!" she pointed out, showing Honey one of them. "This card shows a herd of buffalo in Custer State Park just a few miles from here. We may see them before it gets dark if we start now. I'll write my card when we stop for the night."

"Come on, then. We have a lot more traveling to do before we stop anywhere." Honey hurried Judy back to the car. "You drive, and I'll hold the map. Just keep on along this road, and we'll soon be back on route sixteen."

"This isn't a very good road," Judy commented after five minutes of driving. "Just look at the snow-drifts. I expected there'd be snow on the mountain peaks, but not on the roads in May. We're driving right into winter. Look at those beautiful snow-capped mountains up ahead."

"I'm looking. They're almost blue, aren't they? And see over here at the right. We're even closer to Mt. Rushmore. This is the best view yet."

They were close. A snow-ridged peak loomed directly ahead of them. Nature herself seemed to have done the carving here. Ridges of snow appeared in the likeness of an old man with white whiskers. George Washington, too, had snow on his head and massive shoulders.

"Lincoln isn't quite finished," Judy observed, "or is that more snow drifting over him? I want to get off this snowy road before dark. If the car skids up here . . ."

There was no need to finish the sentence. One look into the gorge below was enough. Above, the serene faces of the Presidents became more shadowy, and a rumble was heard as if they were still echoing the word, "Strangers!"

"Did you hear that?"

"A rock broke loose down there, I think. You turn right here," Honey announced when they came to a fork in the road.

"This is better." The new road was clear of snow, but it still seemed to Judy that they were driving farther and farther into the wilderness. There were no other cars on the road. Nothing could be seen except snow-capped peaks and dark fir trees on either side. Floodlights went on, and again they had a good view of Mt. Rushmore.

"I saw those floodlights up at the lodge where we had those buffaloburgers. Honey, I can't understand it," Judy said. "We should be farther away from Mt. Rushmore than this. Are you sure we're on route sixteen?"

"If you turned left we are."

"Didn't you say to turn right?"

"I said right and then left."

"I did turn left, but this is all wrong," cried Judy. "I don't know where we made the mistake, but we're getting nearer and nearer to Mt. Rushmore and we should be getting farther away. There's a road sign. It's sixteen all right, but we must be going in the wrong direction."

The Presidents' faces appeared in gigantic proportions at the next turn. They startled Judy. She gasped,

"Oh, no!" and there was a distinct echo. The faces were still on Judy's right.

"You see," Honey pointed out, "we are turned around. We must be. The mountain shouldn't be there. It's a lake on the map."

"We'll go back then, as soon as it's safe to turn."

Judy waited until they had passed through a rock tunnel. Now she was sure they hadn't been on this road before. They would have remembered anything as unusual as that. She turned the car in what Honey said was the proper direction and returned under the same tunnel. Through it she could see the floodlights on the faces of the four Presidents and on that strange other face created by the snow. They were just as near as ever.

"We can't seem to get away from them. It's uncanny, isn't it?" she asked.

Honey laughed. "Weren't you the one who wanted to see Mt. Rushmore?"

"I've seen enough of it to last me for the rest of my life," declared Judy.

She drove on for a little while in silence, feeling the strangeness of her surroundings even though the road was the same one she had traveled before. The headlights picked up reassuring 16 signs and an arrow pointing ahead to Custer, a town that was clearly defined on the map.

"There'll be a motel or tourist cabins there. I think we ought to stop," Honey said. "It's too dangerous driving over these snowy mountain roads at night."

Judy agreed. But, somehow, they did not seem to be making much headway. Half an hour later they were still within sight of Mt. Rushmore with the Presidents' faces now on their left.

"This isn't the right road either!" Honey suddenly exclaimed. "There aren't any more sixteens, and we're coming into snow again. Oh dear!"

"There's a number!" Judy looked at it in amazement. "What are we doing on route eighty-seven? How did we get here?"

"I don't know," replied Honey. "Maybe we took another wrong turn, but it's all right. I remember a route eighty-seven going south almost parallel with route sixteen. Either road will take us to Custer."

"You hope!" Judy was still driving, and Honey was still holding the map although it was too dark for her to see it. Something had happened to the lights inside the car so that it was impossible to turn them on. Honey fumbled around in the glove compartment for the flashlight Judy usually kept there.

"Where's your flash?" she asked. "I want to check. Maybe I forgot something on the map."

Judy sighed. "Maybe we both did. This road is awfully narrow for a main highway."

"It isn't a main highway. It's a short cut."

"Did you say a short cut? It's the longest short cut I ever saw. Look, Honey! It's going right through that rock up ahead. See the square opening. Oh!" Judy exclaimed.

There, as they entered the rocky tunnel, was another magnificent view of Mt. Rushmore with the flood-lights still on it. Honey couldn't understand it. "We can't drive this far and get nowhere. That mountain should be out of sight by now. This isn't the same rock tunnel—or is it?"

"It can't be," Judy said. "The mountain isn't quite as near as it was then. We're gradually getting away from it. I just didn't realize there'd be so many twists and turns."

"Can you see your watch?"

"No, but it must be late. We're passing some beauti-ful rocks," Judy observed. "You can see them like tall church spires against the sky. It's too bad we had to drive through here at night. Now we're coming to another tunnel—"

"No, it's the same tunnel! There's Mt. Rushmore again."

"A different view, but we're no farther away than we were before. That's strange. I guess we're really lost," Judy admitted. "It looks to me as if we're off here in the wilderness going around in circles with the road getting narrower and narrower all the time."

"It is narrow. Oh, Judy! Watch it!" Honey cried out in alarm. "We're crossing a natural bridge, and it's so narrow the Beetle could slip right off!"

CHAPTER XIV

Civilization!

"WE MADE IT!" Judy breathed a sigh of relief when they were across. It did seem to be a natural bridge with water rushing somewhere in the gorge below. An animal peered out at them. They couldn't see what it was. They could only see its eyes like two bright sparks in the dark.

"I hope it's—friendly, whatever it is," Honey said with a shiver.

"Probably it's a deer. Right now I wouldn't care to meet a herd of buffalo, would you? It is scary along here," Judy admitted. "The snow has melted on the road, but those blobs of it along the banks pop up like ghosts with everything else so black. No wonder they call these the Black Hills."

"What'll we do, Judy?"

"I intend to keep on driving as long as I can," she replied staunchly. "This road is bound to lead us somewhere if only back to Mt. Rushmore. The lodge there would be better than nothing, though I don't suppose they keep tourists. I didn't see any cabins, did you?"

"Not after we turned off route sixteen. Maybe if we try to find our way back we'll find ourselves going ahead. These roads are so contrary. It might work," Honey said hopefully. "Do you think it's worth trying?"

"Right now I'd try anything to get off this narrow road. We have to come out of this wilderness some way. Oh dear! There's a long hill ahead. The Beetle will never make it. We're almost out of gas."

"Try it anyway," urged Honey. "We can coast down the other side."

Jagged outlines of rocks in curious shapes showed themselves against the sky from time to time. One looked like the eye of a giant's needle. Patches of snow showed ghostly white against the blackness of the night. The hilltop was miraculously reached and passed although the gas tank registered empty. Halfway down the slope, through the dark evergreens, appeared a glowing dot of light. Honey saw it first.

"Civilization!" she shrieked in such an ecstasy of delight that Judy began to laugh.

"It's an electric sign of some kind. We must be

coming into Custer, though I don't think I'll ever know how we got here. Look, Honey! There goes a car on a main highway. If we can make it to the intersection we're saved."

The Beetle just about made it. Without gas, it ran on its own momentum to the foot of the slope and a little way beyond. But, at the next rise of ground, it stopped as much as to say, "I've had it. Now you're on your own."

The light was still there. It served as a beacon as the two girls left the car at the side of the road and began walking. The night was clear and cold. A thousand stars were twinkling above the dark fir trees that lined the road. There were no more strange rocks and no more sudden views of Mt. Rushmore. It was a long walk, but Judy kept steadily on. "We need the exercise after sitting in the car so long," she said to encourage Honey, who was beginning to fear the light was an illusion. There was nothing else to indicate that they might be near a town.

"What's that!" Honey stopped abruptly and screamed when an animal darted out from the bushes and started to follow them. Then Judy saw it was only a cat hunting in the woods the way Blackberry often hunted in the woods at home.

"If there's a cat, there are bound to be people not too far away," she reassured her.

Soon she could make out the dim shapes of the buildings ahead. There seemed to be several of them, but only one was lighted. Another car went by along the main highway. It didn't stop. But it was proof that people existed. Finally they came to the welcome marker at the crossroads.

"It's sixteen! We're back on our own route," exclaimed Honey. "If these people sell gas we may still make it to Yellowstone by four o'clock tomorrow afternoon."

"I wouldn't count on it." Judy had noticed an "A" after the number 16 on the marker. "It may not be our route after all," she said, "but we can look at the map and ask directions if the people don't shut the door on strangers."

"Let's go there, anyway." Honey was running along beside Judy, chattering to keep up her courage. Both girls knew there was a chance that they might be turned away.

Walking was easier on the main highway. Dark trees now hid the buildings and made both girls feel that they were still in the wilderness. Rounding a bend, they came upon a roadside cabin, locked and deserted. Honey was dismayed.

"What happened to that light we saw?"

"It didn't come from this cabin. See that square building showing white against the hillside? I think the light was there, but they've turned it out. After all, it is night. People do turn out lights when they go to bed."

"They won't like to be waked up."

"I know," Judy said, "but we'll have to chance it. We'd freeze out here all night."

They struggled up the path to the square white building. It turned out to be a filling station as well as a restaurant, closed at this hour. The light had come from an electric sign proclaiming the one word, EAT. Finding no bell, Judy knocked on the door of the adjoining house.

"Please, somebody!" she called when there was no answer. "Let us in. We need gas."

That brought a response. A light flashed on. The door opened, and a woman in a flowered housecoat and ridiculous nightcap peered out at them and said to her husband farther back in the shadows, "Land sakes, Pa, it's a couple of girls!"

"We went up to Mt. Rushmore and then we got lost," Judy told her. "We've been driving for hours and not getting anywhere. I don't know what we did wrong, but we kept going around in circles."

"The scenic route," the woman said. "That's for sightseers."

"We couldn't see very many sights in the dark," Judy continued. "There were several tunnels through the rock and a natural bridge—"

"The Needles! Don't tell me you came along the Needles drive at night! Why, that's dangerous even in the daytime. Pa, did you hear that?"

"I heard." The man she called Pa appeared in a striped bathrobe and said, "Come in! I'll open up the restaurant and make you some coffee."

"You're kind, awfully kind," Judy told him, "but if you can just give us a room for the night and let us have some gas in the morning so we can get started—"

"Tell me," Honey broke in, "do you think we can still make it to Yellowstone tomorrow?"

"Might," he said, "driving all day. Ma, we got a room made up?"

"Not in the house," she replied. "One of the cabins is ready. It's cold, though. I'll light a fire and warm it up for you. Just a minute. I'll slip on my coat."

"Did she say one of the cabins? There must be several of them," Honey whispered. "This could be the place—"

"How many cabins do you have?" Judy asked. "We only saw one."

"There's more out behind the trees. Six in all. We do a good business in the summer. My name's Bertha Johnson, by the way. I guess I ought to take your names. I've been suspicious of strangers ever since last fall when these four people came and left without signing the register. It wouldn't have been so bad if they hadn't left the boy—"

"We heard about that." Judy's eyes met Honey's. Without trying, they had found the cabin where Kevin had been abandoned. She was about to tell Mrs. Johnson that the little boy was now living in her own house when a thought flashed through her head. Perhaps the Wheatleys didn't want it known. She remembered how glad they had seemed to find the house in Dry Brook Hollow was so secluded. "As if they were hiding him," she thought, not at all pleased at the thought that her own house was being used as a hideout.

"That was a heartless thing to do," Mrs. Johnson continued, leading the way to one of the cabins as she talked. Inside was a fat heating stove that gave out warmth almost immediately. The cabin contained a double bed, a dresser, a washstand with bowl and pitcher, a row of hooks on the wall, and the little stove.

"Is this the cabin where the little boy was left?" Judy questioned.

"No, it was that one down by the road. It's a double cabin. The two men had one side, and the man and his wife shared the other. I didn't see the boy when they rented it. He must have been asleep in the car. People do that sometimes, try to hide their children so they won't have to pay extra, though goodness knows I charge little enough. You girls can have this whole cabin for five dollars with the use of the showers and house out back. Where's your luggage?"

"Back in the car—"

"Well, then, I'll lend you two nightgowns. Pa won't mind walking to the car in the morning to put in the gas and check the oil. He's done it lots of times. It's when people take advantage of us that he gets riled up. That couple with the little boy, for instance. He was crying so hard I couldn't find out who he was at first. They'd left his clothes but no toys of any kind, and he kept crying for his Teddy bear. We hunted a bit. By then he'd calmed down enough to tell us his name. We notified the police, and they located an aunt and uncle who were willing to take him. Far as I know he's still with them. His ma and pa never did come back."

"When was this? Do you remember the date?" asked Judy, trying not to appear too curious.

"Sure I do," Mrs. Johnson replied. "It was the night after the bank was held up. That's what I mean. If they had signed the register it might have helped the police locate them." She thrust a worn notebook before their faces and said, "You girls better sign before I leave the cabin."

CHAPTER XV

Forewarned

"Didn't she make you feel guilty, as if the police were after us or something?" Honey asked after Mrs. Johnson had left them alone in the cabin.

She had signed their names, *Grace and Judy Dobbs, Farringdon, Pa.*

"I always feel like somebody else," she confessed, "when I sign my real name. You named me Honey, remember? I've been so many people."

Honey was thinking back to earlier experiences before she found out who she really was. It seemed strange to Judy that there had ever been a time when the shadow of a secret hung over the Dobbs family.

"And now we may change names. I'm Mrs. Peter

Dobbs, and you may soon be Mrs. Horace Bolton," Judy laughed.

"Who said so?" Honey demanded, flushing up to the ears.

"I did. I was just wishing—"

"Your wishes," Honey interrupted, "have an uncanny habit of coming true. You wished we could find the cabin where Kevin was abandoned, and we did. If you want to wish something, why don't you wish we'd find the handsome Mr. Nogard?"

"Done," said Judy. "I wish we'd find him. I did tell Peter about him on the last card I sent. You know, just mentioned his name and said we might see him again when we get to Yellowstone. Nothing to worry him. I must write another card first thing in the morning."

They bolted the door, though it seemed unnecessary, and began to undress. The borrowed nightgowns were much too big. Lost in hers, Honey was soon asleep. Judy studied the atlas she had thought to bring with her when they started walking. Now that she had light she could see exactly what had happened. She hadn't noticed it before, but there were two branches to route 16 joining again to make a circle. Both were red roads on the map. Between them, winding in and out among the Black Hills, were a number of little blue roads, some with numbers and some unmarked. No wonder they had gotten lost without the map to guide them. The red roads joined again at Custer. From there the route went straight across Wyoming without any treacherous scenic roads to confuse them.

"We can make it," Judy told herself, closing the atlas. Honey had carried only her tote bag with the unopened package inside. It no longer tempted Judy. "We'll know what's in it tomorrow," she thought just before she dropped off to sleep.

The sun was just rising when Judy awoke. She tiptoed over to the window and looked out. Then she looked again, unable to believe the beauty she saw. Her first thought was, "I must tell Peter."

She had purchased a giant postcard of Mt. Rushmore to send him. As soon as she was dressed, she stepped out into the clearing around the cabins to view the scenery. Then she seated herself at a picnic table and began to write:

"Dear Peter: We rode the dinosaurs on the card I sent yesterday, and then we drove up to Mt. Rushmore and saw the National Monument just as it is pictured on this card. You would have loved it. We had buffaloburgers in the cafeteria and then drove on through the Black Hills and really got lost. We kept going around in circles and kept seeing Mt. Rushmore. The floodlights were on it, but everything else was dark. The road went through a number of rock tunnels and over a natural bridge. At last we found an overnight cabin. Honey is still asleep in it, but I woke up early and came out here to watch the sun rise. It was here that Kevin was left alone. If the Pringles were going to abandon him, they couldn't have picked a

more beautiful spot. From where I'm sitting I can see
wild, rocky scenery in every direction. This has all been
so unforgettable I wish you could have come with us.

Love forever,

JUDY"

"Are you ready?" It was Honey's voice behind her.
"Don't you think we ought to get started?"

"You're up and dressed!" Judy exclaimed, turning
around. "I thought you were still asleep. And here
comes the Beetle! How nice of Mr. Johnson to walk
down there and put gas in it. I gave Mrs. Johnson the
keys last night. She says they're always up early."

"Breakfast, girls!" There was nothing unfriendly
about the call that came from the square white building. Beside the door, the Johnsons had luminous pink
rocks for sale. They were to be found in the nearby
hills. "Nice for fish bowls," Mrs. Johnson explained.

"We keep cats, not fish," Judy told her, and again
she thought of Kevin and wondered how she would
ever persuade him to give up Blackberry.

"Tell me more about that little boy and his parents.
Did the two men who were with them seem friendly?"
Judy asked.

Mrs. Johnson had to think about this for a moment.
"They did and they didn't. It was all on the surface,
if you ask me. They were very polite. I didn't see any
guns on them, but the woman did have a strange look
in her eyes. It haunts me yet."

She described the two men as young and good-look-ing, not at all the criminal type. "But you can never tell about strangers," she added. "Pa says this is a dangerous business. You never know who you're keeping over-night. But me, I like it. Gives me a chance to practice the Golden Rule."

"You've both been very kind," Honey said warmly.

Judy thanked them, too. She was thinking of her own house and wondering if the Wheatleys thought she had been kind. She had left Blackberry with Kevin, but she hadn't been very gracious about it.

Later, when they were on their way, with the generous lunch Mrs. Johnson had packed, Judy said, "I keep thinking of Blackberry. I do hope he's all right."

"Don't worry about him," Honey said. "He'll be all right. Kevin won't hurt him."

"Sometimes little boys who have been hurt do hurt other things to release their bad feelings," Judy began. "I—"

Honey laughed. "Stop worrying. Now, I'm going to drive all morning and give you a rest. Then we can switch over, and you drive this afternoon. With our lunch all packed, we won't need to stop."

"Where did you put the lunch?" Judy was afraid they had forgotten it, but Honey told her it was in her tote bag along with the mysterious package. They had reached Custer, the last town in South Dakota, and were now on their way to Wyoming, where the

Black Hills leveled off and became desert land with only a ridge of mountains the color of ashes to break the monotony of sagebrush and sand. Driving was easier now. The Beetle sped along, making good time all the way across Wyoming. It stopped only once at a gas station where the girls changed places. Judy was driving now.

"Cody is the last town before we get there." She looked at her watch. "I'll have to drive a little faster to make it by four."

Cody turned out to be a real western town, the kind the girls had often seen on the screen. It was a temptation to stop and buy western outfits displayed in all the stores as they drove through. Cowboys on horseback were everywhere. On the range just outside the town they could be seen herding cattle. Honey hadn't seen any buffalo, but this, she said, made up for it. Wyoming was full of surprises.

"We're nearly there. Wouldn't it be just our luck to find the east gate closed? There is a lot of snow," observed Judy as the Beetle climbed higher.

"Brr! Winter again!" shivered Honey. "You were right about its being cold in Yellowstone."

In spite of the snowdrifts at the side of the road they found it clear all the way to the west gate. There a man in the uniform of a park ranger stopped them to ask their names and how long they intended to stay.

A fifteen-day permit was purchased, and then Judy asked, "How far is it to the Dragon's Mouth?"

The ranger looked at her. Judy was sure she saw suspicion in his face. "Are you sure you want to go there?" he asked. "There are no conducted tours this early in the season. Not all the areas around Crater Hills are protected, though the Dragon's Mouth is roped off. It's one of the older hot springs."

"Older hot springs?" Honey questioned, puzzled. "Do you mean there are some new ones?"

"Yes, indeed," he replied. "New hot springs break out frequently. There's the Black Dragon's Cauldron, for instance. It's a terrific mud geyser about a quarter of a mile up the hill from the Dragon's Mouth. It erupts with such force that tourists are advised to stay away from it. The Mud Volcano is another unprotected danger spot."

"Where is that?" asked Judy.

"Not far from the Dragon's Mouth," was the answer. "Follow this road to Yellowstone Lake, cross Fishing Bridge, and then turn right on the Grand Loop Road. It's open all the way to the Mammoth Hot Springs and the geyser basin. You'll surely want to visit Old Faithful?"

"The famous geyser? Of course we will. It sounds exciting, doesn't it?" A delicious shiver of expectation went down Judy's spine. Honey squeezed her hand and said, "We'll have fun, you'll see. You'll be glad we came."

CHAPTER XVI

A Bear Hunt

AFTER another warning to keep away from the trail leading up to the Black Dragon's Cauldron, the ranger continued giving out information about Yellowstone, the National Park Service, and its regulations. Among them was a warning not to feed or molest the bears.

"It's best to take pictures from your car," he advised. "Otherwise the bears may follow you looking for food. Besides, they're apt to be dangerous in the spring when the cubs are young."

"We haven't seen any bears so far," Judy told him. Bears were the least of her worries, she thought. She explained that they were in a hurry as they had an appointment to meet someone at the Dragon's Mouth.

"It wouldn't be Dan Hill from the picture shop, would it?" he asked casually.

"Dan Hill?"

Honey nudged her and whispered, "*He* said Dan."

"Why, yes," Judy replied. "That's his name." She was relieved to hear that he was from a picture shop. That didn't sound too sinister. Probably it was a package of pictures they had been carrying.

"He'll wait," the ranger said. "If you miss him you'll find him at the shop." He pointed it out on a large fold-out map in the guidebook Judy purchased. It was almost like the one that Dale had consulted when he found a picture of the Dragon's Mouth. The map was much more complete than the one in the atlas.

"You see," continued the ranger, "how the Grand Loop Road goes around in the shape of a bear. Here's Fishing Bridge near his paw. You turn right there and drive about five miles. The Dragon's Mouth is on the upper side of the road. After you've seen it you may want to drive on to the Grand Canyon. The river is high at this time of year, and the falls are at their best. The scenic road—"

"No scenic roads, please," Judy interrupted, in a hurry to be on her way. "We were lost on one in the Black Hills. We prefer to stay on the Grand Loop Road."

The ranger smiled. "I was going to tell you the scenic road to Artist Point will give you the best view of the falls. If you're here to take pictures you may want to stay at the Canyon Hotel or Lodge. The cabins aren't open, but if this warm weather keeps up they soon will be."

"Did he say warm weather?"

Judy and Honey laughed about it as they drove on. It seemed cold to them. It looked cold, too, with snowy peaks in every direction. Brilliantly colored wild flowers were blooming beside the snowdrifts deep in the hollows. Rivulets flowed from the melting snow and lost themselves on the green slopes.

A lake, high up in the mountains, looked as if it had once been the crater of a huge volcano. Coming down from the heights, Judy felt the same popping in her ears that she had felt on her first airplane ride. Now steam seemed to be rising from the snow on the lower side of the road.

"Are those the hot springs? How strange!" Honey exclaimed as more steam vents came into view. "I didn't think they'd be like that. They look a little dirty."

"They're just muddy, I guess. That whitish stuff isn't snow after all," Judy observed. "It must be some sort of chemical deposit from the hot springs."

Honey looked at them with distaste. "I hope they don't erupt. We were warned against some mud geyser. What did he call it?"

"The Black Dragon's Cauldron. I wonder what it's like."

"It can't be too dangerous if there's a trail up to it. I've never seen a geyser," Honey said a little wistfully.

"Old Faithful won't be muddy," Judy predicted. "The steam is pure white in pictures. I'd like to see it, but not today. We can't even stop at the lake butte for a good view of Yellowstone Lake."

"We can see it from here. How still it is! And yet you can hear a sort of roaring as if it were growling at us." Honey shivered.

"Maybe it's warning us." Judy was driving along the rim of the lake, mystified by the sound that came from it. She would have thought it was thunder if the sky hadn't been a cloudless blue.

At Fishing Bridge, Judy turned right as she had been directed. There were buildings along the lake's edge, but soon they were out of sight. Yellowstone River rushed along, deep in the gorge on the lower side of the road. On the upper side were dark trees that reminded her of the trees in the Black Hills.

"I hope we don't get lost again," Honey began.

"How could we? This map shows everything, even the hotels and stores. We're in the woods now, but I still don't see any of those ferocious bears we were warned not to molest. It's just silly—"

"Is it?" Honey interrupted. "What's that up ahead?"

"It *is* a bear!" Judy exclaimed. "No, it's two bears, a big one and a little one. Isn't the cub cute the way it follows along behind its mother. It's a temptation to stop and take a picture."

"Too late!" Honey said. "There they go off on the hill. I'll get your camera ready, and we'll take a picture of the next bear we see."

"You take it," Judy told her. "I don't believe we'll see any more bears. We're nearly there."

"And I'm nearly starved." Munching sandwiches in the car hadn't been too satisfactory. "Aren't you hungry?" Honey asked.

"A little," Judy admitted, "but I can wait. We'll be ready to walk around and see the sights by the time we get to the Dragon's Mouth. We'll be ready to eat, too. There's some food left, I hope."

Honey peered into her tote bag to see, but before she could answer, Judy cried out excitedly, "Oh, look! There's another bear. Isn't he cute? What a shame Kevin couldn't see the bears in Yellowstone. This one is little and black just the way he described his Teddy bear."

"He can see him if we take his picture. There's time for a quick snap of him." Honey rolled down the car window and aimed the camera at the bear. "You'd think he was posing for this picture, the way he sits there beside the road. Now he's begging like a puppy. I didn't know bears were so tame."

Judy told her the Yellowstone bears were famous for being tame. "He's begging for food, but we were warned not to feed the bears. Snap his picture fast, and I'll drive on."

"Poor little fellow," Honey sympathized. "I know how he feels. I'm hungry, too. There are two sandwiches and a box of cookies left in my bag—"

"And that bear knows it. Watch it, Honey!"

Honey snapped the picture, but she wasn't quite fast enough. The little bear's nose was in the window and her tote bag was being hauled out of it before she quite realized what was happening. Judy leaned over in a vain attempt to snatch it away from him. Too late! The little bear galloped off with his prize between his teeth.

Honey snapped the camera shut and opened the car door. "He's got my bag! Make him give it back, she cried unreasonably.

"Drop it!" screamed Judy, but of course the bear paid no attention.

"We'll have to follow him. Come on!" Honey grabbed her hand saying, as they ran, "Who ever thought this trip would turn out to be a bear hunt?"

"There he goes up the hill!" Judy pointed. "Isn't he funny? He doesn't want your bag, Honey. He just

wants the cookies. Why doesn't he stop and eat them?"

"He's looking for a safe place."

"Up here?"

The hill seemed far from safe to Judy. She had noticed the spongy appearance of the ground almost at once and, as they followed the bear farther up the slope, it became more apparent. It wasn't easy to catch a bear. It wasn't easy to run, either. The hill was dotted with treacherous little craters from which steam escaped. Honey noticed it, too.

"Are we on one of the crater hills?" she said. "There's a thin crust of mud over everything, and that stream I just jumped across was hot. Here, let me take your hand. If one of us breaks through the crust—"

"Don't bother. You'll lose that bear."

Honey ran a few feet and then stopped. "I'm afraid I've already lost him. Did you see which way he went?"

"Up that trail, I think!"

Honey darted ahead. Somewhere, in the back of Judy's mind as she followed, the warning sounded, "Keep away from the trail up to the Black Dragon's Cauldron." Was this it? She could see why the ranger had called it dangerous. But she did not stop until a shower of black mud gushed fully twenty feet into the air and descended upon the path directly ahead of her. Then she stopped so abruptly that she nearly fell.

"Honey!" she screamed. "Are you all right?"

An answer came from the hollow beyond the geyser. "Yes, I'm still following the bear."

"Let him go and come back here," Judy cried. "I've turned my ankle, and this crust is so thin I'm afraid I'll make another geyser if I move. Oh dear!"

"What?" asked Honey, hurrying back. She circled the erupting geyser and then stared at Judy. "What happened to you?" she asked in amazement. "You're all spattered with mud."

"Don't come any nearer!" Judy cried. "I did break through. This black mud is sucking me down!"-

CHAPTER XVII

A Mud Volcano

"HERE, grab this!" Honey tore at an overhanging branch and bent it down toward Judy. She grabbed it and swung up, Tarzan-like, almost into the tree. Breathless, she hung there for a second while Honey stared at a new geyser erupting in the very place where Judy had been standing a moment before.

"I—I made that one," Judy managed to say. "That's where I broke through the crust."

"Are we safe now?"

"I don't know, Honey." Judy could see that they were standing on what looked like the rim of a large crater. The whole area was dotted with smaller craters and cracks from which steam escaped as if something were cooking in a great kettle just below the surface of the earth.

"It's a volcano. That's what it is. Maybe it's beginning to be active again. Let's get away from it fast," Honey suggested.

"I'm afraid I can't get away—fast." Judy was trying to conceal the pain she felt when she tried to stand.

"Why not?" asked Honey.

"I can't! Oh, Honey! I'm trying, but I can't even stand up with my ankle hurting so. That mud was hot. Help me to a safer place, and I'll take my shoes off. I think I burned myself."

Honey helped Judy to a rock that looked solid, and they both sat down. They huddled together for a moment comforting each other. Then Honey found snow on the shady side of the rock and bathed Judy's burns. They weren't deep, but they did smart. There were red splotches on her face and arms and a rim of red around her burned ankle. Her shoes, thick with evil-smelling sulphurous mud, were quickly removed and cleaned with snow.

"They'll dry in the sun," Judy said. "Just let me sit here a minute and clean the mud off my suit. I'm a mess. I would have to discover a geyser the hard way." Judy rubbed the mud off the face of her watch and saw the time. "Five o'clock!" she exclaimed. "We didn't make it."

"We'd be there now if we hadn't stopped to take a

picture of that bear. He ran off with our lunch, but do you know what else was in my bag?" Honey asked.

"That package for Mr. Nogard!"

"Yes, and all my traveler's checks. Judy, I have to find that bear and get them back. He's probably stopped by now to eat the cookies and sandwiches. He may have torn the package open—"

"The way we hoped the kitten would."

"Judy, do you know what this means?" Tears were in Honey's eyes. "It took will power not to open that package. Now we may never know what was in it."

Judy hadn't thought much about the package except to tell herself it wasn't hers, and anything belonging to anyone else was private. That hadn't taken will power. It was part of her nature.

"We'll find it. We just have to," she said. "If we can't, we'll have to meet Mr. Nogard and tell him—"

"Tell him what?" cried Honey. "Do you think any man in his right mind would believe we drove all the way to Yellowstone to return a package and then let a bear snatch it away from us? We're in enough trouble without meeting him and trying to explain it."

"What will we do then?"

The question begged for an answer. Something had to be done—and soon. The immediate danger was over, but nothing seemed really safe in this wilderness of new sights and sounds. Behind them the crater of the great mud volcano gave forth a hissing sound as the violent action of its geysers gradually subsided.

"They'll erupt again," Honey predicted. "We ought to get out of here before they do." She pointed to the enormous crater where the great mud geyser was still spouting its black liquid. "If that is the Black Dragon's Cauldron, I can see why we were warned to keep away from it, can't you?"

"Even the lake warned us."

The strange rumbling sound she had heard still mystified Judy. There was so much to see in Yellowstone, so much to make her wonder. Why must it hurt her so to walk? It was no use pretending. After the first few agonizing steps Judy knew she could not possibly keep up with Honey.

"Please go ahead," she begged. "This trail leads to the Dragon's Mouth if we follow it back to where it begins. Mr. Nogard or one of his friends may be there to help us. I can't make it back to the car alone. I'll hobble along slowly. You run ahead. Please, Honey!"

"All right, Judy." Honey brightened again at the thought that she might still meet Mr. Nogard. The ranger had said Dan Hill would wait for them, too. "They'll think we're Cookie and her sister, but I don't care. I'll tell him the whole story after I know him better."

She meant Mr. Nogard, of course. Judy could see that Honey was still interested in the handsome stranger. She thought of Horace and compared them in her mind. Her brother was an idealist, always quoting and living by the words of great thinkers. What was

Mr. Nogard, and how did he live? Had he named himself Nogard to frighten people when they discovered his name was Dragon spelled backwards?

"Honey, I've just thought of something," Judy said slowly. "If Mr. Nogard does belong to a gang of some kind who call themselves the dragons and meet at the Dragon's Mouth—"

"Theories!" Honey interrupted. "You know what Peter always says. You can't accuse anyone of a crime until you have the facts."

"I know. I want the facts, too," Judy admitted, "but in the meantime—Honey, do be careful."

Honey laughed. "How can anyone be careful in a place like this? I won't fall into the Dragon's Mouth Spring if that's what you mean. It's supposed to be roped off."

"I mean—be careful of Mr. Dragon."

"You mean Nogard."

"It's all the same. I just don't trust him," Judy said.

"Well," Honey retorted, "he helped us once, and maybe he'll do it again. You take your time, Judy. I'll run ahead."

"All right then. I'll try to keep up."

Judy had found a stick which she used as a cane. She felt like an old woman hobbling along with one shoe in her hand. Her ankle was swollen all the way down to her toes. She felt pain at every step.

"Be careful going down this hill. Don't slip!" Honey called back to her.

There were bushes along the trail that Judy could grasp if she did slip. The trail itself was packed hard.

"Are you all right, Judy?"

Honey was not too far ahead of her. Judy felt, vaguely, that they ought to be together in case of sudden danger. But she couldn't ask Honey to wait.

"I'm all right," she called back bravely. "I'm coming as fast as I can."

The trail snaked this way and that to avoid the hot spots. It was downhill all the way. Judy limped along cautiously, afraid of creating another geyser with the stick she was using as a crutch. She knew the dangers of leaving the hard-packed trail, and yet she felt she would have to leave it if she saw the bear or the remains of Honey's tote bag and its mysterious contents.

"We can't give up and not even look for it," she thought as her eyes searched the bushes on either side of the trail.

Soon she came to a terrifying crater filled with bubbling black mud. If it ever erupted . . .

"Judy!" Honey's voice broke in on her thoughts. She was calling from far ahead along the trail. "You were right about where this path leads. See that steam! Hear the roaring noise! I think I'm coming to the Dragon's Mouth. Ah, there's Mr. Nogard—"

Honey's voice trailed off. Judy thought she heard another voice, but she wasn't sure. She could see the steam now, and the roaring noise became louder. It drowned out all other sound.

CHAPTER XVIII

An Odd Discovery

LIMPING faster in anticipation, Judy soon came to a clearing that gave her a good view of the scene ahead. The picture in the guidebook had not done the Dragon's Mouth justice. It had not shown the scaly greenish-colored rock with bushes growing on top to form ridges on what appeared to be a dragon's back. The dead branches of an ancient tree made it look as if the creature had an eye that seemed to wink at Judy.

"It's only the wind blowing the branch," she told herself to still her growing fear.

Now she could see the gable-shaped promontory of rock that formed the dragon's long nose with the crater below appearing to be a wide open mouth. A flashing tongue of boiling water and steam darted in and out, in and out, with a thumping rhythm that never stopped.

"It must go on like this day and night. How long will it continue?" Judy wondered and the word *forever* seemed to be thumped out in answer to her question. The continuous pulsating and thumping deep in the cavern accounted for the roaring sound that increased as she limped nearer.

"Honey!" she called and heard only her own echo as it was thrown back from the dragon's mouth in another burst of steam.

Then she saw it—a bit of black off there in the brush that formed the ridges on the monster's back. Could it be the bear hiding and eating his feast of sandwiches and cookies? But why was he so still? Was it a bear after all?

Judy had to find out. Climbing up there would be difficult with one foot almost useless. But she had to do it. The hope that she might recover Honey's lost bag and return Mr. Nogard's package encouraged her. Finally, crawling on her hands and knees, she was up the rocky ledge. She could feel the steam rising about her from the Dragon's Mouth now almost directly beneath her. It was like warm breath against her face.

"I am afraid," Judy admitted to herself, "but I'm not going to give up."

Names like the Dragon's Mouth and the Black Dragon's Cauldron had been chosen for these hot springs because of the fear they inspired. But they inspired something else, too. It was with a feeling of awe and wonder that Judy gazed on the thumping pool of boiling water in the cavern now directly below her. If she fell—but she would not fall. She knew how to climb, and she had to see if that black thing really was the bear they had followed.

As she crawled farther out on the rock she could see that it was in the shape of a bear, but still it did not move. It hung limply over a branch with its head flopped over to one side and its bright button eyes wide open.

"It doesn't look alive," she thought, reaching for it. "It looks—why, it *is!* It's a Teddy bear—*Kevin's* Teddy bear! No other bear would be made of black caracul. But why is it ripped open?"

This question brought other questions to Judy's mind. She looked long and searchingly at the sodden Teddy bear she had practically risked her life to rescue. She was using her head now. She was thinking fast. And the more she thought the more alarmed she became. This was Kevin's Teddy bear. She was certain of that. But he hadn't lost it here, because he had never been to Yellowstone.

"Someone must have stolen it just the way he said," Judy thought, "but why? Was something hidden inside the Teddy bear?"

Most of the stuffing was gone, and there was a long

If she fell—but she would not fall

rip down the bear's middle as if some hidden treasure had been taken out and the bear carelessly thrown away.

Poor Bumper! He did not look like a bear that had once been loved and cuddled. His ears did stand up like Blackberry's, even now. What else was it that Kevin had said? "Daddy told me not to lose him." And there was something still more important. "He told me to put a candy heart in him to make him alive." Then Kevin's father knew the bear's secret, and now Judy feared she knew it, too.

"The Wheatleys were right," she thought. "Kevin's parents did take part in that bank robbery. And they hid their share of the loot in the bear!"

The shock of this discovery unnerved Judy so much that she could hardly steady herself enough to climb down from the overhanging rock. Holding on to the Teddy bear, she eased herself a little way backward—and then slipped! For one agonizing minute, she was sliding—sliding down the slippery green rock toward the steaming pool below.

"Help!" she screamed.

But Honey did not come to help her, and neither did Mr. Nogard. Judy managed to help herself by catching hold of a branch. Finally, without quite knowing how she did it, she brought both herself and the Teddy bear safely down to solid earth.

"Whew! That was an experience!" she exclaimed

aloud as she brushed herself off and tried to stand. It was no use. Her ankle was swollen worse than ever, and now it was bruised as well. But she had the bear. Eager to show Honey her discovery, she picked up the stick she had been using for a crutch and limped on down the slope. She looked for Honey in vain. There was no one at all beside the steaming hot spring known as the Dragon's Mouth.

Now Judy was really frightened. The rhythm of the exploding steam beat in her ears, reminding her of Indian drums beating out some fantastic ceremonial dance. That thumping and roaring noise must have kept Honey from hearing her call for help. The steam itself could be hiding her from view. She *had* to be there! Judy had distinctly heard her say, "There's Mr. Nogard." But now, as a gust of wind blew the steam upward, it revealed nothing—nothing at all. Judy couldn't understand it.

"Honey! Honey!" she called, but the echo from the cavernous mouth of the dragon was her only answer. A fantastic thought came to her. "He's swallowed Honey." But she knew the dragon, like the Teddy bear in her arms, was not alive. He could do no harm. Only the steam thumping forth from the rock was real and dangerous. The appearance of a dragon was just an illusion. From this angle the cavern hardly looked like a dragon at all.

"Honey!" Judy called a little louder.

"OO-NEY!" the cavern echoed in such a hollow roar that Judy knew she must get away from it before she called again. Honey wasn't there. That was certain. If she had really seen Mr. Nogard, she had probably followed him—or followed what she thought was Mr. Nogard. That could have been an illusion created by a burst of steam from the Dragon's Mouth. If Honey went too near— But there were ropes to keep people back. The hot spring was protected so that a person could not accidentally fall in except from the rock above . . . "Where I was!" Judy shuddered as she thought of her narrow escape. Honey couldn't have seen her up there. The bushes would have hidden her from view just as they had hidden the Teddy bear. As for Mr. Nogard, Judy doubted that Honey had seen him at all. Realizing she was alone, she must have hurried off immediately for help.

"I'll wait here and think things out. She's bound to come back for me soon," Judy told herself bravely. But, with every fresh burst of steam from the Dragon's Mouth, new fears swept over her.

CHAPTER XIX

A New Fear

JUDY had a lot of thinking to do. Maybe, if she really used her head, she could figure out exactly what happened the day the Rapid City bank was robbed. The Teddy bear was a clue. Peter would be glad she had found it.

"He said he'd look for it," she thought, "but I'm sure he didn't think it would ever be found. I'll take it back home with me . . ."

But when she thought of home, tears came to Judy's eyes. Home seemed so far away. It was lonely here by the hot spring with only a Teddy bear for company. Who had stolen it and thrown it away? Had the thief, whoever he was, aimed for the boiling pool of hot water and missed? Judy shuddered at the thought. Anything that went down in that boiling water would never come up again—never! No wonder the Wheatleys thought it was dangerous to take Kevin to Yellowstone.

"Maybe one of the bank robbers threw the bear away," Judy decided. "Perhaps the Pringles were afraid of them."

Mrs. Johnson, at the tourist camp, had said the look in Peggy Pringle's eyes still haunted her. Had the Pringles been forced to take part in the robbery? Why, then, had they accepted a share of the loot? Had one of their so-called friends found out where they had hidden it and stolen the bear in the night? No, that didn't make sense. Nothing did except that something valuable must have been hidden in the bear.

"Something valuable was in the package, too," Judy thought. "If that was Mr. Nogard at the Dragon's Mouth, he may be angry because we lost it."

Judy sat forlornly beside the hot spring, trying to think things out. She heard a car passing. The road must be nearer than she had thought. "Honey may need help more than I do," she reasoned. "I can't just sit here waiting. I must get back to the car!"

Determinedly, Judy picked up her stick and began her painful journey. There were no dangers along this path, although she could see more steaming craters off in the distance and could hear the roar of the Dragon's

Mouth long after it was out of sight. The sun was low
on the horizon. Soon it would be dark.

"Honey is lost," Judy thought. "She must be.
Maybe she and Mr. Dragon are both lost."

She couldn't help calling him "Dragon" in her mind,
because that was what he had become. Fear of him and
of what might have happened to Honey limped beside
her all the way back to the car. Judy wished she had
never met him, never followed him. For that was what
she had done. She had followed him the way Peter
followed men he was assigned to investigate.

"Peter would have stopped me if he had known, but
I deliberately deceived him telling him all about the
trip and leaving out the important part—that package.
We'll never find it—never! Oh, what has Honey told
him? Where can she be?"

When Judy finally reached the car, she thought it
sat waiting as patiently as Blackberry used to wait for
her on the porch at home. The car had never looked
so good. She opened the door and then gasped at her
own reflection in the overhead mirror.

"My face!" she exclaimed. "I can't drive anywhere
looking like this. I'd scare people. Now when did I
do that?"

She was looking at a long scratch that went the
length of her cheek. It wasn't deep. Neither were the
small red splotches that gave her the appearance of a
girl just breaking out with the measles. There was a

smudge on her nose and streaks all over her face. Her jacket was torn in several places, and her mud-spattered skirt could not be worn again until it was cleaned and mended.

A spring of warm water smelling strongly of sulphur helped Judy repair some of the damage. The minerals in the spring also soothed her burns. She bathed her feet and ankles and found she could wear a pair of soft slippers she had brought with her. Her muddy shoes she left on the floor of the car. She slipped on a fresh sweater that she took from her suitcase, and in its place she deposited the Teddy bear, closing and locking him in. A little powder, a little lipstick, and a hasty combing of her auburn curls did wonders for her appearance. Snuggled in her warm car coat, she was on her way. Too late, she remembered that she should have left a note in case Honey did come back.

"We'll be looking for each other all over Yellowstone," she thought.

The National Park was not the busy tourist center she had imagined it. So far, she had seen more bears than people. The bears appeared briefly, then retreated into the dark forest where snow still lay deep under the trees. The Beetle's headlights made the road look white, too. In one place it came so close to the Yellowstone River that Judy could see the foaming rapids and glimpse two small islands washed by spray. At any other time she would have been enchanted by the scenery, but now her one thought was to get help and tell her story—a story she felt certain no one would believe.

After passing the scenic routes to both the upper and the lower falls, Judy came at last to a parking field and a group of low buildings that looked inhabited. Lights gleamed whitely from the windows, and the welcome sign CAFETERIA hung just above the front door.

"Food!" breathed Judy, entering and seating herself on a stool.

"We're just about to close," the woman at the counter informed her coldly. There were only two other customers at a nearby table, and they were nearly finished with their meal.

"Please," begged Judy. "I just want a hamburger and coffee, and directions to—to someone who can help me. I'm afraid my friend is lost."

"Where was she last seen? Or is this friend a man?"

"No, a—a girl. She was with a man, I think. Do you know a Mr. Nogard?"

The waitress shook her head. "Never heard of him. You need the park rangers to help you. I can see you've been too near one of the geysers. You were limping, too. Ah, there's Mr. Hill!" A man of medium build with a wisp of a mustache on his upper lip and a deep dimple in his chin had just entered the cafeteria.

"This girl needs help," the waitress told him. "Do

you have any first-aid equipment in your shop?"

"Sure!" He walked closer, peering at Judy. "Is this the young lady who's been hurt?"

"Don't mind me!" Judy cried. "My friend—I mean my sister is missing. I hurt my ankle, and she went ahead to meet a Mr. Nogard at the Dragon's Mouth. You know him, don't you? You are Mr. Dan Hill?"

"That's my name," he replied. "Yes, I know Nogard. He conducts tours here in the summer. If your friend is with him she's safe. You can bank on that. Which is she, friend or sister?"

"She's both," Judy exclaimed warmly. "I wouldn't want anything to happen to her."

The waitress brought Judy's hamburger and two coffees, one of which was for Mr. Hill. He hadn't ordered but, apparently, she knew what he wanted. Judy looked at him closely. He seemed to be well liked, a man that anyone could trust.

"So you're worried about your sister? Tell me more. Why did you come here?" he asked.

"You won't believe this," Judy said, plunging into the story, "but I came to deliver a package. We drove, taking turns of course, all the way from New York. I live in Pennsylvania."

"Farringdon?" he questioned.

She nodded, wondering how he knew.

"So that's where you met Mr. Nogard? What was in this package you came to deliver?"

"I don't know. It wasn't mine."

"But you opened it. You saw what was in it?"

"No, I—I didn't. I thought it might be something personal. I was going to give it back to Mr. Nogard."

"Why did he give it to you in the first place?"

"I think," Judy said, aware that this was going to sound fantastic, "it was because I had a—a corsage of snapdragons."

He lowered his voice. "Wasn't it arranged that you should wear snapdragons?"

"Not me," Judy protested. "The girl at the airport. He called her Cookie. No, I mean he called me Cookie—"

"So you're Cookie? Well, hello," Mr. Hill said, his dimple deepening as he smiled. "I've been wanting to meet you, but what about this sister? Does she want a job, too?"

"She wants *help*," Judy cried. She threw her hands out in a beseeching gesture, her half-eaten hamburger in one and her coffee spoon in the other. "Can't you understand me, Mr. Hill? I came here for help. Please call the park rangers or someone who will look for her!"

CHAPTER XX

The Lost Package

Mr. Hill sat there at the counter stirring his coffee and watching Judy. He seemed undisturbed by her frantic plea for help.

"My dear Cookie," he said at last. "I am sure you believe that your sister is in danger, but I can't call out the rangers without a better reason than you've given me. You say this friend or sister, whichever she is, met Mr. Nogard at the Dragon's Mouth?"

"I think she did." Judy decided she might as well let him call her Cookie if it would bring help any faster. "I told you she ran ahead of me. I heard her call out, 'There's Mr. Nogard,' and after that I didn't see where she went. If she met him they may be off in

the woods somewhere looking for that package I told
you we came here to deliver."

"Was it lost?" His voice had an edge to it that should
have warned Judy of trouble.

"It was stolen by a bear. You see," she went on
recklessly, "we had it in the bag with our lunch and
when we stopped to take a picture of him, this—this
bear ran away with it." She hesitated, sensing his disbelief. "You see the way it was? We didn't mean to
lose it."

"I'm afraid I do see." He finished his coffee and rose
from the stool. "Suppose we go over to my store
where we can talk in private. Then you can tell me
what really happened."

"But I am telling you!"

He shook his head. "Not here. I'm interested in your
story, but I want it straight. Then, if you're still determined to call in the rangers, I'll get in touch with
the park superintendent at Mammoth Springs. He's a
personal friend of mine."

Hoping that Mr. Hill would be willing to help her
find Honey, Judy allowed him to assist her to his store.
Like the cafeteria, it was a low building covered with
brown shingles. Behind it, Judy could see a group of
cabins. None of them seemed to be occupied.

"Are those cabins for rent?" she asked. "When we
do find Honey, we have to look for a place to stay."

"So her name's Honey?"

"That's what I call her. It's just a pet name."

"And you're Cookie?"

Before Judy could answer, a cry came from one of the dark cabins. Judy shivered.

"Wh-what's that?"

Mr. Hill seemed undisturbed by the wail. "We often hear unexpected noises in the park, thunder over the lake when the sky is clear, and wails from empty cabins. I'm told it's static electricity—"

"How could static electricity make a noise like a human cry?"

"You can't explain these things," he replied. "It could be a trapped animal."

"Why not a trapped human being? I think we ought to investigate—"

"My wife will look into it later," he said, hurrying Judy toward his store and unlocking the door. He snapped on the light, and at the same time music sounded from somewhere behind the counter. Near the windows were the usual racks displaying post cards and souvenirs and a group of chairs for waiting customers. Judy was helped to one of them and told to make herself comfortable. Mr. Hill pulled up a footstool.

"Thanks," Judy murmured. "Dad says you should keep a swollen ankle elevated until the swelling goes down. He's Dr. Bolton of Farringdon. That's what I've been trying to tell you. I'm not Cookie—"

"Why, then, were you wearing snapdragons?" he interrupted.

"I saw *her* wearing them. She was at the airport waiting for Mr. Nogard. I know, because she had him paged. I liked the corsage she was wearing and ordered one like it. Then, quite by accident, I met Mr. Nogard, and he mistook me for her and gave me the package."

"And then a bear snatched it away from you? Is that what you want me to believe?"

"It's the truth!" Judy cried. "I want you to believe it because it's the truth. A bear did snatch the package—"

"Wait a minute!" He held up his hand. "Calm down and think what you're asking of me. You've heard the story of the boy who cried, 'Wolf!' Well, here it's much the same. If you call out the rangers when they aren't needed, you may find yourself calling in vain when you're in real trouble."

"I think I am in real trouble," Judy insisted.

"You will be if that package isn't found," Mr. Hill declared. "You can't leave it off in the woods where anybody can pick it up."

"Do you know what's in it?" Judy asked in surprise.

"Don't you?" he countered.

"I told you it was given to me by mistake. I didn't open it. Can't you understand that I wouldn't open a package that wasn't mine? I intended to return it to

Mr. Nogard. I suppose he must be angry because we lost it. Was it anything important, Mr. Hill?"

"The rangers will think so if they get hold of it before he does."

"But you will call them, please? You do have a telephone, don't you?"

"In there." He indicated a door Judy had not noticed before. "It leads to my office. I take care of mailing out pictures and other paper work where I won't be disturbed by customers. My wife looks after the shop in the daytime. She'll fix you up. Oh, Agnes!" he called, and footsteps were heard from one of the rooms in back of the store.

"Agnes, this is Miss Bolton from Pennsylvania, or so she tells me. See that she's made comfortable, won't you? Cabin number six. You understand?"

A look passed between them that Judy didn't like. There was something artificial about Mrs. Hill's whole appearance. She was not a woman Judy would have turned to for help or sympathy.

"Can't I stay right here until my sister is found?" Judy pleaded. "The rangers will want a description—"

"Very well," Mr. Hill agreed without waiting for Judy to finish. "I can see you've had quite a day. In the morning I may ask you to go back there and point out the direction that bear went. How's the ankle?"

"Better," Judy said. "It helps to rest it."

"Keep it elevated and try not to worry too much

about your sister," Mr. Hill advised. "As I told you,
Mr. Nogard knows his way around. She can't be lost
if she's with him. They are probably driving around
in his car looking for you."

"Of course," Judy agreed quickly. "They're probably just as worried as I am. Isn't there some way to
get in touch with them?"

"The rangers will locate them if I tell them it's
urgent. And now," Mr. Hill finished politely, "if you
will excuse me, I'll put through the call while my
wife takes care of your ankle."

Confident that everything possible would be done
to locate Honey and the elusive Mr. Nogard, Judy allowed Mrs. Hill to put some kind of soothing ointment
on her burned ankle.

"There's soda in that hot spring by the road. It was
clever of you to think of it. You know quite a bit about
Yellowstone, don't you?" Mrs. Hill asked as she bathed
Judy's face with the professional detachment of a
trained nurse.

"I wish I did," sighed Judy. She leaned back in the
chair and closed her eyes. "I am tired," she admitted,
"more tired than I knew."

She was dozing when she became aware of a con-
stant pounding noise. It was like fists beating against
a closed door.

"What's that?" she exclaimed, starting up with a
cry.

Mrs. Hill was nowhere about. Her husband hurried in from the back of the store.

"Is something wrong?" he asked solicitously.

"That noise—"

"You must have been dreaming," Mr. Hill interrupted, dimpling. "I didn't hear a thing."

Judy listened a moment. Now she no longer heard the noise. "Perhaps it was a dream," she admitted. "How long have I been asleep?"

"A couple of hours. There was no need to disturb you," he continued, still smiling. "The rangers located Mr. Nogard. You were right. He and the girl you call Honey were looking for the package just as you thought. You should have waited for them."

"I know. I'll tell Honey I'm sorry. Where is she?" Judy asked eagerly.

"She's asleep in one of the cabins. You will be together soon."

What a funny way Mr. Hill said it, as if they would not like being together! Mrs. Hill came in and motioned to him.

"Go with my wife," he advised. "She will search your bags. Perhaps the package was not lost in the woods, but among your possessions. Wherever it is, we intend to find it."

CHAPTER XXI

Locked In

"You mean—you think I hid it?" Judy was trying to collect her thoughts, arrange them in some order. "If I hid the package, why would I come all the way out here to tell you about it?"

The question seemed to puzzle them.

"You have some motive. Money, probably. If you were sent here by some private detective agency, you're probably being well paid for it. There will be papers in your bags to prove why you came here."

"I see. So you think I'm a detective?" This pleased Judy at the same time it frightened her. She thought of the Teddy bear she had hidden in her suitcase. Her bags must not be searched until she knew who had ripped it open and thrown it away, and why. Most of all, she wanted to know why.

"You are afraid the rangers will find that package before you do, aren't you?" she asked. "Did you call them, or were you only pretending? If my bags are to be searched, I think the park police ought to do it."

"You see," Mr. Hill said, turning to his wife. "Isn't that what I told you? If I didn't know they were all men, I'd think this girl was one of the government's bird dogs. Nogard said she'd been trailing him. He suspected a trap would be set for him at the airport."

Then it was true! It was all true. There was a dragon gang, and they were all involved in whatever they feared she was trailing them to discover. Her thoughts flew to Honey. Was she really asleep in one of the cabins, or had some harm come to her?

"Were you telling me the truth?" Judy demanded. "Is my sister safe?"

"She's safe," Mrs. Hill replied, "but we don't think she's your sister."

Mr. Hill smiled. Judy could see now that his dimpled smile was evil. How could she have thought him to be the well-liked storekeeper everyone seemed to believe he was?

"You will come with us," he said. He still sounded courteous. But Judy knew it was an order. Perhaps the wisest thing would be to obey it.

"Very well," she replied, trying to sound submis-

sive, "I'll come, but first I'll have to get my bags.
They're in the car."

"That won't be necessary," Dan Hill informed her
still in that over-polite tone. "There is no need for you
to carry your own luggage."

"But you said—"

"I said my wife would search your bags," he broke
in more sharply. "They will be brought to your cabin
after they've been searched—not before. We can't take
any chances."

Judy smiled. She couldn't help it. Didn't they know
they were taking the worst chance of all when they
broke Federal law in the first place? For she was sure
they had broken it. Only lawbreakers would speak of
government men so contemptuously as bird dogs.
She thought of Peter. Bird dog indeed! She wished he
could smell out these evil birds and discover what they
were doing.

"You will come with us."

The order was being repeated. Judy suspected Dan
Hill had a gun in his pocket to make the order
more emphatic if necessary. She came, not knowing
what else to do. She did want to see Honey. And so
she walked, with Mr. Hill on one side and Mrs. Hill
on the other. They crossed the grassy yard to the
last cabin in the row behind the store. Unlocking the
door, they pushed Judy inside.

The push was so unexpected that she fell and lay

stunned for a moment. It was Honey who helped her to her feet. At first they were too surprised and relieved to speak.

"Honey, you are here!" Judy sobbed as she hugged her. They told me—"

"Watch it!" Honey cried, but she was too late. The door had closed. They both knew it was locked, and now Judy knew something else. It had been Honey crying and pounding on the cabin door while Judy slept. They had known where she was all the time!

"You must have had a terrible time. What happened to you after you ran ahead of me?" Judy asked. "I heard you call out that Mr. Nogard was there. Why didn't you come back and help me?"

"He wouldn't let me," Honey said. "He's mean, Judy. First he thought I'd come to him for a job of some kind. Then he made me traipse all over the hills looking for that horrid package. I wish I'd never told him we had it. That—that package caused all this trouble."

"Do you know now what was in it?" Judy asked, sitting down beside Honey on the bed where she had been sleeping.

"No, I still don't," Honey replied. "Do you?"

"I'm beginning to get an idea," Judy told her. "I found something at the Dragon's Mouth. It's in my suitcase. When they let us out of here I'll show it to you. Why do you suppose they've locked us in?"

"It may be a trick to get us to talk. Be careful what you say," warned Honey, "in case they may be listening. They're the dragons," she added in a whisper. "They hire people to commit crimes, and that's why they thought I wanted a job."

"I guess you convinced them that you didn't."

"Yes. That's why I'm here. I could have pretended, but I'm no good at it. They would have given me a job in a bank—"

"A bank they were planning to rob?"

"I—I guess so. They didn't tell me that. They just asked me if I'd had any experience, and when I told them I was an artist they said, with a knowing look at each other, 'We have jobs for artists, too, if you turn over that package.' What did they mean, Judy? What were they trying to get me to do?"

"Forgery, probably."

"Oh dear!" Honey's eyes widened. "What makes you think so?"

"I just put two and two together." Judy had other reasons, but she didn't dare mention the Teddy bear for fear they would hear her. They couldn't know she'd found it, and they couldn't search her suitcase until she gave them the key. It was on the chain with her car keys and both were safe in her coat pocket—or were they?

"Honey!" she cried out in sudden panic. "My pocket's empty. They've taken my keys. They must have gone through my coat while I was sleeping. I did doze in the chair and now they have my car keys as well as the key to my suitcase. We have to get out of here before they open the suitcase and find my discovery. It links them to the Rapid City bank robbery, but Honey, it links Kevin's parents, too. I have proof, but they'll find it and destroy it. We have to get out of here and stop them!"

Honey picked up a chair.

"There is a way. I thought of it before, but breaking glass makes a lot of noise and I didn't dare. We could smash this chair through the window."

"No!" Judy protested. "We'd cut ourselves, and the noise would bring them running. We might better loosen the putty and take out the glass."

"I thought of that, too, but the putty's on the outside. Even if we did get out," Honey added gloomily, "we'd be stopped before we got halfway across the parking lot."

"I know," Judy agreed. "My ankle is still swollen. I'm afraid I can't run very fast."

"What'll we do then?"

"Something will turn up. How much did you tell them?" asked Judy. "They must really have it in for us. Mr. Hill said something about the government's bird dogs, and I knew he meant Federal agents. Do they know about Peter?"

Honey shook her head. "Not from me."

"They have their own grapevine, I guess. They're certainly planning something—"

"A getaway!" Honey exclaimed. "Isn't that the Beetle's motor?"

"It sounds like it. We can't stop them, but the rangers can. Keep back, Honey! I'm swinging with the chair, and then it's out the window for us. There's a telephone in his store and in the lodge, too, I think. You run for it as fast as you can."

Honey made some reply, but Judy couldn't hear it. As she swung the chair forward, there was a sound of breaking glass—and then it seemed to her as if the sky itself had descended upon her. She saw stars, and then everything dimmed into darkness.

CHAPTER XXII

Hungry Bears

"Speak to me, Judy! Please speak to me!"

Honey's voice finally penetrated Judy's dream. It was something about Kevin. He had his Teddy bear, and it was Blackberry Judy had found on the ridge above the Dragon's Mouth where someone had thrown him and left him hanging . . .

"Oh, no! It was a Teddy bear!" Judy exclaimed, still wrapped in the fog of her dream.

"What was a Teddy bear? Wake up, Judy! You're all right. The glass fell outside the window. You aren't cut or anything. It was a clean break—"

"What hit me then?"

"It was the window shade. It fell and knocked you

dizzy, I guess. You didn't even try to get up. I'm sure you're not hurt. It was only the window shade."

"So that's what it was." Judy sat up on the floor and began to laugh. "Oh, Honey! I thought the sky was falling and I was going to tell the king. We'll have to tell somebody—fast. I didn't dream we heard them stealing the Beetle, did I?"

"No, you were dreaming about a Teddy bear."

"That wasn't a dream, either. Seriously, Honey," Judy began, "I did find a Teddy bear ripped open and thrown away on that ridge above the Dragon's Mouth. I saw it and thought it was the bear we were following, and so I climbed up there. When I saw what it was I was so surprised I nearly fell in the pool. I'm sure it's Kevin's Teddy bear."

"In Yellowstone? How could it be? Didn't you tell me he never got this far?"

"I know, but he described the Teddy bear and it was just the way he said. Someone did steal it and probably forced his parents to take part in the bank robbery as well. They'd hidden the money inside it, and that's why it was stolen. I'm not sure, of course, but it does make sense."

"Does it?" asked Honey. "I had just about decided that the money was in that package we carried all the way across the country and then lost. Why else would they be so eager to find it?"

"They said they were going to search my bags, and

we have to stop them. They're probably members of a nationwide gang who call themselves the dragons. Mr. Nogard is probably the head—"

"No, he said he gets his orders from Mr. Hill. He said I would, too. He really thought I'd help him."

"You will help him in the long run if you get him behind bars before he kills anybody," Judy said grimly. "He was armed, wasn't he?"

Honey began to tremble. "He didn't have a gun. He had a knife. He said he used to throw knives at a carnival and he never missed."

"He missed if it was he who threw away that Teddy bear," declared Judy. "I think he aimed for the pool. He didn't want it found. I'm sure of that. If he sees it in my suitcase—"

"He mustn't. We have to stop him before he does."

"I know. Honey, I'm still dizzy when I try to walk. You run ahead and telephone."

While they were talking Honey had placed the bed covers over the window sill and managed to climb out without cutting herself on the broken glass. Now she stood shivering outside the cabin. Nights were cold at this altitude even in the summer, and it was only the first week in May.

"I'll run around in front and let you out through the door. Don't try the window," Honey advised, and Judy waited while she tried the door. It had been bolted from the outside.

"You go ahead." Judy leaned against the frame of the open door trying to overcome her dizziness. "The telephone in the store is nearest. If they've locked it, smash another window. The rangers will forgive us. You go ahead, Honey, and hurry!"

"No," Honey said firmly. "Look what happened when I did that before. We stay together this time."

"Agreed." Judy took a deep breath of the clean mountain air. "There! That's better. I guess I can walk all right with you to lean on."

She didn't say so, but her ankle was no better. Actually, it felt worse, but she limped as fast as she could. They reached the store, but it was in darkness. Daylight was just tinting the sky.

"Listen to the birds!" exclaimed Honey. "They don't mind the cold. They're peeping and twittering their little hearts out, and the sky is all pink. Oh, Judy! Take a minute to look around you. Isn't everything beautiful?"

"It is," Judy agreed, "but Mr. Hill won't stop to admire the scenery—not in a stolen car. I'm sure the store is locked, but we'll try the door anyway."

"It's locked," Honey announced, leaving Judy without support for a moment while she tried it.

"I knew it would be. Those windows in back lead to his office. They're probably locked, too."

Honey picked up a stone and broke a portion of the window glass.

"There! Now I can reach in and unlock it," Honey announced. "I didn't cut myself, either. We've been lucky so far . . ."

Her voice faded away. Judy swayed dizzily and caught herself. The window was open now, and Honey was inside. She found the light switch first and then the telephone. Judy heard her clicking the transmitter buttons up and down trying to get a dial tone. "Lucky, did I say?" Honey's voice ran on. "The wire's dead. I can't get a sound."

"It's been cut." In spite of her dizziness, Judy was quick to observe the dangling wire. "We'll have to try the one in the lodge. That's where the cafeteria is. I hope I can walk that far."

"It didn't seem so far before. They told me you were in the cabin, and I was so eager to see you. Then," Honey continued as they began their walk under the dark trees, "they pushed me in and locked the door, and I knew they'd been lying to me. Judy, you're still dizzy!"

"Maybe it's the altitude. I'm used to hills, but not mountains. They're sort of majestic, aren't they? I suppose we may as well take time to admire the scenery," Judy agreed. "It looks as if we're stuck here for a long, long time."

"I'm afraid you're right," admitted Honey. "With your car gone and our suitcases and even my bag with all my cash and traveler's checks lost, we're pretty much at the mercy of the next person we meet."

"There isn't a human being around anywhere that I can see," observed Judy as they started across the parking lot, now empty of cars.

"There must be a caretaker or someone at the lodge," Honey said hopefully.

Judy shook her head. "I'm afraid not. They've made sure we wouldn't get help in time to stop them. We're almost to the lodge. We can try banging on the door when we get there."

"Let's!" cried Honey. "I feel like banging on something. It's all my fault for being so taken with the handsome Mr. Nogard. You were right, Judy. Handsome is as handsome does. Right now our brothers—yours and mine—would be about the most handsome sight in the world. I'd love this trip if they were with us, but alone—"

Judy shivered. "Are we alone? I hear something back there in the woods, and it doesn't sound like birds. Oh dear! It's getting louder. What is it?"

"Bears," Honey gasped as they came into view. "Look, there's a whole family of them, and they're coming right toward us. Run, Judy, if you can! Hungry bears are dangerous."

"What's that?" gasped Judy as they ran, holding fast to each other. A crash as of something falling had sounded from somewhere back of the lodge building.

Soon three bears appeared. One was dragging something while the other two growled and snarled. Honey banged frantically on the door under the sign that said CAFETERIA.

"Help!" she and Judy both cried out at the top of their voices.

They had forgotten, for the moment, that here, where their car had just been stolen, the people might be more dangerous than the bears.

CHAPTER XXIII

A Long Wait

"We'll have to break in again if no one comes." Honey pounded on the door again and called, "Help! Help!" just as another crash sounded from back of the shingled lodge building.

"Someone's back there!" cried Judy. "That's a familiar sound. Don't you recognize it? It sounds like someone lifting the cover of a garbage can to empty trash. Let's go back and see."

"That someone could be a big grizzly. No, thank you," Honey said. "I'm staying right here until someone comes. Look! A light went on. Now, both together!"

"Help! Help!" both girls shrieked even louder than before.

"Be patient. I'm coming," a woman's voice called from somewhere inside, and presently the door opened just a crack, then all the way. The waitress who had served Judy the evening before stood in the opening.

"What on earth is the matter?" she exclaimed. "If you stay in your cabin, the bears won't hurt you. They're around here all the time, tipping over our garbage cans and eating the leftovers."

"We know," Judy said. "It isn't the bears. We want to use the telephone. It's an emergency."

"I'm sorry, but the telephone is out of order. Mr. Hill said he'd report it—"

"He's stolen my car!" Judy interrupted.

The waitress looked at her as if she were mad. "Mr. Hill? Stolen your car? You must be mistaken. He left in his own car for the ranger station at Mammoth Springs. Mrs. Hill went with him, but they said they'd be back in time to open the store. This is the best time of year for photographers. I can see you two girls found each other. Are you here to take pictures?"

"That's one of the reasons," Judy said shortly.

"Well, you can have them," the woman replied, smiling. "I don't care about photography. I'm just one of the savages."

"Savages!"

"Employees. That's what people call us," she explained. "I thought you knew. Mr. Hill is an employee too. He started as a pearl diver."

"And worked up to bigger things, I suppose?"

The waitress laughed. "Oh, yes, he's a picture wrangler, now. A pearl diver is Yellowstone lingo for a dishwasher. His wife was a heaver. That's another name for waitress. I took her place when she went to work in the store."

"How long has Mr. Hill been a—a savage?" Judy asked.

"Several years, I think. Anyway, longer than most of them. They start drifting in early in June, college students mostly. Cabin girls are pillow punchers, and the seasonal park rangers are ninety-day wonders. When they arrive, this place really comes to life. There's nobody here now but the Hills and me. I'm Katie Hubbard. The young heavers all call me Mother Hubbard, and I'm afraid my cupboard is pretty bare but I can offer you something. I was a little short with you last night when you came in alone, Miss—"

"Just call me Judy."

"Well, as I was saying, Miss Judy, something had upset me. The rangers stopped by, and you'd think they were investigating me, all the questions they asked. Then they quizzed the Hills—"

"They did?" Judy was curious. Honey was sitting beside her at the counter not saying a word.

"That was before you came," Mrs. Hubbard continued. "Afterwards, well, I began to get nervous about it.

"I'm a widow, you see," she went on. "My husband was killed accidentally. At least, that's what I thought at first. Afterwards, I began to have my doubts, but I didn't say anything. It's best to keep quiet until you're sure."

"Sure of what?" Judy inquired.

"Well," she admitted, "lots of things go on that folks can't explain. Noises in the night. Take last night, for instance. I was sure I heard someone crying. I asked Mr. Hill about it, and he said it was static electricity like that noise over the lake. This was more of a wailing sound."

"That was you crying for help, wasn't it, Honey? My sister had been locked in the end cabin," Judy explained. "When I found her there, I knew something suspicious was going on. The Hills locked me in, too. We had to break our way out, and someone did steal our car—"

"Mr. Nogard," Honey put in.

"Who's he? You mentioned him last night, but you can believe me when I say I never heard the name before. I wouldn't blame you two girls if you didn't trust anybody after what went on last night. I suppose this Mr. Nogard is at the bottom of it."

"No, Mr. Hill is," Judy objected. "That's what you told me, isn't it, Honey?"

"That's what Mr. Nogard told me. His name is dragon spelled backwards. He made it up to scare people, and when that doesn't work, he throws knives—"

"Knives!" Mrs. Hubbard exclaimed, her face turning white. "You should be telling all this to the park police. My husband had a knife wound in his back when they took him to the hospital. The doctor told me he died of pneumonia, but it was the knife that caused it. He was stabbed by accident, they told me, but now I wonder. The police will hear of this. I'd call them myself if the telephone was working."

"The wires were cut. It was deliberate," Judy said. "I know now why they locked us in the cabin. We knew too much about them. Mr. Hill told me he'd call the rangers and I believed him, but now I know it was all a trick. There's nobody left to help us but you, Mother Hubbard. Will you?"

"How can I?" she asked. "I have no car, and it's eighteen miles to Park Headquarters at Mammoth Springs. It's a short drive, but a long, long walk. With your bad ankle, you shouldn't try it."

"But we need help," Judy protested. "All three of us need help. If we wait here, do you think maybe someone will come in for breakfast? One of the rangers, perhaps? They do patrol the park, don't they?"

Mrs. Hubbard shook her head.

"We don't see many people up here until June. It's too early and too cold. If this warm spell keeps up, more people will come, but you can't count on it."

"How long will we have to wait before anyone comes?" asked Honey.

"Until noon if nobody else stops in for breakfast. It's Sunday. There may be a photographer or two out taking pictures. The trouble is, they usually come only as far as Inspiration Point and then go back to the canyon. There's a ranger station there and a big hotel—"

"How far away?" Judy interrupted to ask.

"Nineteen, maybe twenty miles. You must have passed it on your way here. It's on the scenic road."

Judy sighed. "Wouldn't you just know it? I avoided the scenic road and missed seeing the hotel."

"Our best hope is that someone else will do the same thing." Mrs. Hubbard set out cups of coffee and joined the girls at the counter. There were sugar doughnuts and sweet cinnamon buns in front of them, but Judy wasn't hungry. The very sight of food gave her a queasy feeling in her stomach. She wondered why. Honey was eating and chatting away as if this were just an ordinary breakfast. Not until an hour later did she say a little impatiently, "It's going to be a long wait."

"Too long," Judy agreed. "I wish I felt well enough to walk." She was lying down on the sofa in the lobby of the lodge building, not even feeling well enough to sit up. Whenever she lifted her head it began to ache. The window shade couldn't have hit her that hard, could it? She tried to think. She couldn't just lie there and let a gang of bank robbers escape in the Beetle. What would Peter say?

"Can't we do something?" she asked. "All three of us know that Mr. Hill isn't coming back. He had no intention of stopping at the ranger station."

Mrs. Hubbard still doubted that Mr. Hill could have been mixed up in anything dishonest.

"I've always trusted him," she insisted. "You know how people are about a storekeeper, especially if he sells film and gives expert advice on picture taking."

"He's an expert on a lot of things, I'm afraid," Judy said from the sofa. "He isn't taking any chances on being caught, now that we suspect he was involved in that Rapid City bank robbery."

"Just a minute," Mrs. Hubbard objected. "Mr. Hill couldn't have been involved in that robbery. He was right here keeping store all day the day it happened."

"He was?" Judy found this hard to believe.

"The rangers will tell you it's the truth. Look!" Mrs. Hubbard exclaimed, glancing toward the door. "Here comes a patrol car full of rangers now! There must be trouble," she added apprehensively as she admitted four men in uniform.

"There is trouble and plenty of it." The tallest ranger approached the sofa where Judy and Honey were sitting. "We've been looking all over the park for you two girls," he told them. "You'll have to come along to headquarters with us. We have a big surprise waiting for you."

CHAPTER XXIV

A Big Surprise

JUDY didn't ask what the big surprise was. Her dizziness was increasing. Whatever it was, she hoped there would be a place for her to lie down at headquarters. She sat up with an effort, and the room whirled.

"Shall we come now?" Honey asked. "Our car's been stolen. We wanted to report it, but the telephone wires were cut—"

"We know." The ranger spoke quietly as if he knew the whole story. He was one of the permanent rangers of the national park service, he explained. When necessary, he cooperated with other government agencies, including the department of justice.

"Stolen cars are our business," he added. "Yours got

only as far as the northeast entrance, where it was
stopped. The occupants are being held for preliminary
hearing before the park commissioner whose duty it
is to pass sentence. . . ."

His voice droned on. Honey asked all the questions.
When she and Judy left with the rangers Mrs. Hubbard was still protesting that Mr. Hill had nothing to
do with the Rapid City bank robbery. His car hadn't
been stopped and certainly he hadn't stolen the Beetle.
Mr. Nogard and his companion were the thieves.

There was so much to see on the way to Mammoth Springs that Judy didn't want to miss any of
it. Honey kept exclaiming and pointing out unusual
sights—a waterfall, a petrified tree, and many steaming hot springs. Bears came out of the woods as the
patrol car passed, but they were no longer a danger.
Safe inside, Judy could relax and wait for whatever
would happen next. She closed her eyes for a moment,
and the next moment they flew open to see the Ameri-
can flag waving from a flagpole in front of a square,
two-story building with the word, ADMINISTRATION,
over the door. The patrol car stopped. Judy couldn't
believe it when she saw who was there to meet her.

"Peter!" she cried. "It *can't* be you! You're in
Washington!"

He kissed her firmly on the lips. "Does *that* prove
I'm here? I came the minute I got your post card."

"But it didn't say anything," Judy protested. "I

told you all the good things and nothing about the trouble we were having."

"You gave me the name Nogard, and that spells trouble. There are a lot of names for that character and lots of ways to read them. Nogard, by the way, is a made-up name."

"I know. Backwards, it spells 'dragon,' " Judy said.

"School is over in Washington for the present," Peter went on. "There are four of us here to investigate the dragons."

"Mr. Hill is the head. Honey will tell you about it. Peter, where are they taking me?" Judy asked as a man appeared with a wheel chair.

"To the government hospital. Don't worry," Peter said gently. "I'll be right beside you."

Judy closed her eyes, listening to the comforting sound of Peter's voice. Later, in the hospital, her ankle was efficiently treated, and Judy was allowed to leave.

"Peter," she asked, "when are we going home?"

It came as a shock when she remembered that the house was rented. But she couldn't keep Peter here beside her when he was needed elsewhere.

"I'm sorry," she said before he had time to answer. "I'm being selfish—"

"Selfish!" he exclaimed. "Great galloping goldfish! Wait until the chief hears that it was you who smelled out these—"

"The word is birds," Judy put in quickly. "Vultures, I guess. Mr. Hill called the government men bird dogs."

"I've heard that term before. How did he happen to use it?"

"He said if he didn't know they were all men, he would think I was one of them. I did find out a lot I haven't told you. Where's Honey? Did she tell you how we met Mr. Nogard?"

"She did say something about a turtle. Nogard said that's where he made his mistake, stopping to help a couple of girls. But I told him he made his mistake a long time ago. We have him and his companion on an auto theft charge, but we suspect them of bigger things—"

"And I have proof if we could only find that package Honey had in her bag."

"It will be found. That's what we're here for. Chasing bears can be part of our field work."

"Oh, Peter! Be careful," begged Judy. "Don't go near the hot springs. Geysers pop up—"

"Is that what happened to you?"

"Yes," she admitted, "I discovered one of them, but that wasn't my most important discovery. Peter, where's my suitcase?"

"It was taken up to our room in the hotel here, and that's where you should be—resting."

"I can walk to the room, can't I?" Judy asked.

"Not **yet**," Peter said. "Doctor's orders. You still

have a little fever. That burn on your ankle was infected, but it will soon heal. Then we can drive around and see the sights. Our men are at the Dragon's Mouth now, looking for clues—"

"But I have a clue. That's what I started to tell you. I found Kevin's Teddy bear!"

Hardly stopping for breath, she told Peter the whole story of the real bear who had stolen the package Mr. Nogard had given her by mistake, and the toy bear she had found just above the steaming hot spring known as the Dragon's Mouth.

"That's where the dragons met to plan things. I'm sure of it. Anyway, they met there to divide the money that must have been hidden in the Teddy bear. Then one of them threw it away. I know," Judy declared, "because the bear was ripped open and the stuffing taken out and—"

"Wait a minute!" Peter stopped her. "Harry Pringle told me about that bear. We need it to clear him. He said we would find a note in the bear, but first we had to find the bear."

"Oh, Peter, you found Harry Pringle!" cried Judy. "Does the Teddy bear really clear him of the charge against him? I thought it might prove he took part in the bank robbery."

"It proves he was telling the truth when he said the robbers commandeered his car and forced him, at gun point, to drive it to a secluded tourist cabin—"

"We stayed there, Peter! I told you about it on a card. We can stop there again on the way home, and you can question Mr. and Mrs. Johnson. She told me the look in Peggy Pringle's eyes still haunted her. They must have left Kevin there so he wouldn't be hurt, but I don't know who found out the note was inside the Teddy bear and came back and stole it in the night. Will we discover that, too?"

"We sure will," Peter said. "With that little old Teddy bear to help us, we may force a confession out of Nogard. Or our lab may tell the story if the cutting was done with his knife. Think you can sew up the bear when our men get through with him?"

"I'll wait and let Kevin help," Judy decided. "He wanted to put a candy heart inside him. You'll have to visit the Wheatleys officially, anyway, won't you? I hope they understand what happened better than I do. Where were the Pringles all this time?"

"I can't reveal the exact place," Peter replied guardedly, "but I can tell you that they were being held prisoners by the dragons. Harry says he thought they were about to be murdered and so they left Kevin behind and put a desperate appeal for help in his Teddy bear. Peggy wrote it, but apparently Nogard suspected what she was doing. You know the rest. It was just as Kevin said. A bad man stole his Teddy bear, note and all, and left his parents at the mercy of the dragons. They were watched day and night. Harry

Pringle was picked up when our men raided the place in connection with another robbery."

"Mr. Hill probably planned that one, too. Peter, he hires people to commit crimes. I know it. Oh, I hope they find him and make him confess to what he's done. He just sits in his snug little office here in Yellowstone where everybody trusts him and directs crimes all over the country. I found out all about it," declared Judy. "I was mistaken for Cookie and she's a dragon, too. She was going to meet them—"

"She won't now," Peter interrupted gently. "Our men have already picked her up for questioning. We'll stay here a week or two, depending on how long it takes to locate Mr. Hill and get a conviction. After that, wherever I go you go with me. It's a promise, Angel. In the meantime, wouldn't you like to really visit Yellowstone? You haven't seen any of the big attractions."

"Oh, Peter!" Judy exclaimed. "We can have such a marvelous time, and on the way home everything will be twice as beautiful with you to share it. It's only when we get back that it will seem strange. I mean with strangers living in our house."

CHAPTER XXV

Strangers No More

It DID seem strange at first. After an unforgettable two weeks in Yellowstone and an equally wonderful trip home, Judy, Peter, and Honey arrived in Farringdon. Dr. and Mrs. Bolton's house on Grove Street was their first stop.

"I'm glad you're home safely, Judy girl," Dr. Bolton said seriously. "Just because you're married, don't think your mother and I no longer worry about you."

"I wish you wouldn't, Dad. I'm all right, and I did help Peter. I was helping him all the time and didn't know it, and all because I wore a corsage of snapdragons!"

There was so much to tell that Judy and Honey both talked at once. Horace was there eager for news. It wasn't only because his paper wanted an exclusive

175

story, now that the whole gang who called themselves dragons had been rounded up and convicted. He wanted Honey exclusively to himself.

"Absence made my heart grow fonder," he confessed.

"Mine, too," Honey told him. "I've lost all interest in smooth young men as handsome as that phony Mr. Nogard. Horace, he was the masked gunman who held up the Farringdon National Bank and also helped rob the bank in Rapid City last September. Mr. Hill directed the business, if you could call it that, and saw to it that there was always a girl employee planted there who would hand over the money for a share which Mr. Nogard made it his business to deliver. That's where we came in, wasn't it, Judy? We were so conscientious about delivering that package, and all the time it contained Cookie's share of the stolen money!"

"The rangers found it," Judy added. "You'd never guess where. In a heated cave! Did you know those Yellowstone bears have steam heat in their houses? Well, that was where that thieving little bear dragged Honey's tote bag. They took us up there to see the place. It's all in Peter's report. We were at the hearing, too. Oh, it was quite a trip, but it's good to be home."

Judy turned to Peter and said, "All the way home I've been worrying for fear the Wheatleys aren't the right people to be living in it. We're going there for a visit, Mother. Can you imagine visiting in your own home?"

Mrs. Bolton sympathized. "This is always your home, dear," she said.

As a guest of the Wheatleys the following day, Judy did feel a little uncomfortable. As soon as she could leave the group downstairs without appearing impolite, she hurried up to the third floor where her own and her grandmother's things were stored. To her dismay, she discovered that Kevin had been into them.

"Mrs. Wheatley!" she called, and the former librarian came quickly to the top of the stairs.

"Yes," she said when Judy asked her about it. "I'm afraid Kevin did disturb the things you had stored up here. I wouldn't have had it happen for anything, and yet, in a way, I'm glad. Judy— May I call you Judy? I knew you as a little girl."

"Yes, of course," Judy said. "I have something for Kevin—his old Teddy bear."

"You found it?" Mrs. Wheatley exclaimed.

"Didn't Peter tell you? There's so much to tell, I guess he didn't have time," Judy said. "A man really did steal the Teddy bear. Kevin was telling the truth."

"I should have believed him," Mrs. Wheatley said humbly. "Children need to feel they are trusted, and Kevin needed that feeling more than most children because he didn't have his parents to reassure him," she continued. "Bob and I tried, not very successfully,

I'm afraid, to take their place. This house has helped, and that wonderful cat of yours has been a great comfort. You do intend to leave him for the rest of the summer, don't you?"

"Should I?" Judy was asking herself the question. "I'll have to think it over. I'm afraid, when the summer's over, Kevin will still find it hard to give up Blackberry. Don't you think his old Teddy bear will take his place?"

Judy took Bumper from the box she had been carrying, and at that very moment Kevin appeared. He stared at the Teddy bear, still minus his stuffing, and then let out one wail after another. Peter, hearing the commotion, mounted the stairs in great leaps.

"What's all this?" he demanded. "Didn't Judy tell you she found your bear in Yellowstone with all the other bears? He went to court, too, as evidence, and helped convict the man who stole him. He may be a little worse for his experience, but an operation will fix him up. Where's that candy heart you were going to put inside him?"

"I—I ate it," Kevin confessed and began to wail louder than ever.

"No matter. We'll put in a valentine."

"Here's a pretty one," Judy said, selecting a paper heart from a box of old valentines her grandmother had saved. "It says, 'I love you,' because hearts are for loving—"

"I want him to have brains for thinking, too," the little boy said unexpectedly.

"Brains? Let's see. Will this do?" Peter began wadding some old paper for brains, but Mrs. Wheatley stopped him.

"Do you know what this is?" she asked. "It's a copy of the *Juvenile Instructor* for 1852. That was before the Civil War. Judy, your grandmother has more than a hundred years of old magazines up here. They would make quite a display at the new library in Roulsville. It has built-in display cases, and I'm to be in charge. If Kevin hadn't crawled into those storage places under the eaves, I wouldn't have known you had any such precious old magazines. Wouldn't you like to display them?"

"I'd love to," Judy said, smiling at Mrs. Wheatley. She no longer thought of her as a stranger. But when Kevin looked up, her smile faded.

"Who cut open my Teddy bear?" he demanded, on the verge of tears.

"The bad man who stole it. We may as well tell him the whole story, don't you think so, Peter?" Judy asked. "You see, Kevin, it was this way. The bad man was a bank robber, and he had a knife. Another man was with him, and he carried a gun. They made your daddy and mother drive them in your car so they could get away from the bank with the money they had stolen. But your daddy isn't a thief. He wanted the money returned to the bank, and so he hid a note in your Teddy bear. He told you to put a candy heart inside the bear—"

"So I'd find the note?"

"Yes, and tell somebody. What did the note say, Peter?"

"It told about the bank robbery and asked that the police be notified," he replied. "The rest of it was a personal note to Kevin telling him always to remember that his daddy and mother loved him and that their love would be with him even if they never saw him again. Kevin, did you know your daddy and mother left you alone in that tourist cabin because they were afraid the bank robbers might hurt you?"

"They did hurt Bumper. Shall we operate on him now?" Kevin asked.

The story hadn't touched him as much as it had Judy. She was eager to meet the Pringles. They were expected that evening. Kevin hadn't been told.

"We'll let them surprise him," Mr. Wheatley decided. "What they did is certainly a surprise to me. I judged them too quickly."

"People are apt to make quick judgments if they don't stop to examine the facts," Peter began, but Kevin interrupted.

"Is my Teddy bear a fact?"

"He's a fact we mustn't ever forget," Peter replied.

When Kevin's parents arrived that evening, Peggy

Pringle looked older than Judy remembered her. Harry resembled his sister, Maud Wheatley. Kevin stared at them a moment and then shrieked, "Mommy! Daddy! I knew all the time that you wouldn't go off and leave me."

Judy turned to Peter and said, "I'm not going to be abandoned again, either. Remember what you promised me when we were in Yellowstone? Well, here I am all ready for my next assignment."

Neither of them knew what it would be. Judy liked not knowing. She liked the thought that the future was always a mystery waiting to be solved, but she did want Blackberry to be there to help her solve it. She thought of the kittens he had fathered and remembered that there was still a little black one that hadn't been given away.

"It's yours to keep," she told Kevin when she delivered it. "You can call it Blackie if you like."

"I like Blackie," Kevin said, hugging the kitten. "I'm going to keep him forever and ever."

Judy smiled understandingly. "He won't be a kitten forever and ever. He will grow up to be a cat like my Blackberry. Cats grow up a lot faster than little boys. But they live to be quite old if you take good care of them."

"Judy knows. She takes good care of Blackberry," Peter said, appearing in the doorway. "He's in the car. Is his mistress ready?"

"Ready for anything," she replied enthusiastically.

She would need the lesson she had learned to solve her next mystery, **THE WHISPERED WATCH-WORD.** As they drove away in the Beetle, Judy looked back at Kevin still happily holding his kitten just as she had held Blackberry when Peter first gave him to her. That gift had led to so much happiness that a strange feeling of contentment came over her.

"Peter," she asked, moving closer to him, "aren't you glad the house is rented for the whole summer? Isn't it fun to share experiences with other people?"

"That's what we'll do in Washington," he agreed. "If the government doesn't pin a medal on you for what you've done, I will," he added gaily. "This time we're really on our way together."

Printed in the United States
119075LV00006B/100/P